Editorial

Both the First and Second World Wars saw the rapid development of new technology as the principal adversaries attempted to defeat or counter the equipment and methods of the other. The reasons for these great advances are fairly obvious – the removal of the financial restraints common in peacetime and the impetus provided by the possibility of advancing the end of the war or of preventing defeat.

These situations were characterised by measure and counter measure; for example, the principal naval developments of the First World War were in the use and design of aircraft and submarines which ran parallel with the introduction of anti-aircraft and anti-submarine tactics and weapons. Similarly, the Second World War saw advances both in offensive and defensive methods, one of the more obvious examples being in the Battle of the Atlantic in which the balance of power constantly swung in favour of either the Axis or Allied powers as new U-boat technology and tactics were countered by new anti-submarine technology and tactics.

Despite the new developments, however, much of the resulting knowledge and equipment represented little more than the initial step in the development process. Radar, initiated prewar, was given high priority for development in 1939 but the need to get the equipment to sea rapidly meant that many sets which would have served as prototypes in peacetime became production sets in wartime. Thus, development was undertaken and teething troubles overcome and evaluated in operational use rather than on a test bench – an expensive but in some ways an ideal method of testing new technology. However, despite five years of war and considerable expenditure, radar was only just entering its high technology stage in 1945.

The same situation applied to most other advanced items such as the German U-boats in which the design of new equipment, armaments, machinery and hull forms combined with war experience had by the end of the war resulted in the production of vessels which, by prewar standards, were highly sophisticated but which were, nevertheless, little more than production prototypes. Fortunately for the Allies, few of these boats were built before the surrender but much of the accumulated knowledge provided the basis for postwar developments in the US, Russian and British submarine forces.

The same situation applies in many ways to standard ship production. The need to build ships quickly resulted in early war construction being of the utility type – usually as simple as possible and utilising prewar technology. Thus the USA more or less froze its ship designs in 1942 in order to simplify mass production by employing standard types. It was not until the requirements in ship numbers had been fulfilled that attention was turned to more advanced designs incorporating war experience and necessarily requiring longer design and production times. Thus the British concentrated initially on the production of the 'War Emergency' destroyers (eventually totalling over 100 ships) before turning their attention to the more sophisticated 'Battle' class of the 1942 programme. It is significant that all but about fifteen of the Emergency destroyers were completed prior to the end of the war while only five 'Battles' commissioned and only one of those was early enough to be employed operationally.

The end of a war invariably brings with it not only a return to peacetime standards of expenditure but also a loss of design expertise and skilled labour as personnel return to their normal employment. Thus much wartime development tends to move forward very slowly or stop altogether once hostilities cease. Some idea of the delay that can result can be seen in the British cruisers of the *Tiger* class, completed during 1959-60. They were laid down during 1941-42 to a wartime design and heavily modified postwar to incorporate war experience and new equipment. However, this equipment included an armament and radar outfit which originated in the Second World War. One wonders how long it would have taken to get to sea if the war had continued.

John Roberts

The Type XXI Submarine Part 1

by Erwin F Sieche

When the British occupied Bremen they found dozens of Type XXI submarines nearing completion on the slipways of Deschimag, although some had been damaged by Allied bombing. This photograph, taken on 12 May 1945 , shows (from left to right) *U3051*, *U3049* and *U3055* and, beyond, the *U3052*, *U3048*, *U3054*, *U3056* and, almost hidden among the scaffolding and cranes to the right, *U3057*. *U3052* (damaged) and *U3048* have no bow sections, revealing the domed ends of their pressure hulls with their six torpedo tube openings. All these vessels were broken-up on the slips during 1945-46.

USN, courtesy A D Baker III

Following the heavy losses among conventional submarines during the early part of 1943, the German naval authorities concluded that the existing system of operating conventional diesel-powered 'submersibles' was outdated and should be replaced by the concept of a 'true submarine' capable of high underwater speeds. The *Kriegsmarine* was already developing such a vessel, propelled by an air-independent turbine – the Walter turbine. However, the first prototypes (Type Wa 201, *U792* and *U793*; Type Wk 202, *U794* and *U795*) were far from being tested under operational conditions. It was, moreover, impossible to advance quickly the development of the sophisticated Walter turbine, with its dangerous fuel (High Test Peroxide, $HTP = H_2O_2$), to a position of operational reliability and safety. It was therefore decided, in February 1943, to employ the elegant, streamlined hull of the projected Type XVIII Walter submarine for conventional

propulsion. By using this pressure hull, with its '8'-shaped frames, it would be possible to treble the battery capacity, thus achieving both higher underwater speed and greater endurance.

The catastrophic U-boat losses of March 1943 confirmed that the old types (VIIC, IXC, IXD, etc) could not match existing, and certainly future, Allied ASW techniques, so Dönitz decided that the conventionally powered version of the Type XVIII design should be proceeded with rapidly, and construction began as soon as possible. Designated the Type XXI, it was to replace the old Type IX submarines. They were also known as 'Hertha-submarines', or more simply 'big electric boat' (in contrast to the 'small electric boat', the Type XXIII coastal submarine), after the code-name for their powerful electric motors.

CONSTRUCTION PLANS
The design was completed in June 1943, the projected boat being

Part of the flotilla of operational Type XXIs surrendered to the British at Horten where, during the last weeks of the war, they had been awaiting their orders for the first 'Paukenschlag'. The boats concerned were *U2502* (Franke), *U2513* (Topp). *U2518* (Weidner), *U3401* (Hornkahl), and *U3515* (Kuscher).

USN, courtesy A D Baker III

capable of a maximum speed of 18kts for 1.5hrs or 12–14kts for 10hrs, and a creep speed of 6kts for 28hrs. Initial construction estimates showed that the first two prototypes could not be ready until October 1944 and a further 30 boats could be completed in the autumn of 1945 but that they would not become operational before 1946. This was unacceptable to Dönitz and he persuaded Hitler to give full responsibility for the Type XXI construction programme to the Minister for Armament and Ammunition, Albert Speer, whom he admired for his ability to push through his wishes against heavy opposition. One must keep in mind that at this time a great number of influential people were competing to obtain high priorities for their own development projects or programmes – rocketry, jet-propulsion, radar, new tanks, Atlantic wall construction, V-weapon launching sites, etc. Speer agreed, and adopted a new management scheme – a 'central board for ship construction' (*Hauptausschuss Schiffbau*, or HAS) – responsible for all co-ordination between design bureau, yards and suppliers, which was assigned to Speer's ministry.

The first director of the HAS was the dynamic Otto Merker, former general manager of the Magiruswerke. He was a specialist in automobile manufacture and introduced the modern mass-production assembly-line technique to shipbuilding. His studies showed that one of the major problems when trying to shorten the construction time for a submarine was that there were only a few small hatches through which

workers and materials could enter the hull. He therefore proposed dividing the hull into eight prefabricated sections, which could be produced quickly by different suppliers who were not necessarily skilled in shipbuilding techniques, and then assembled at one of the main shipyards.

More than 1000 engineers and designers, gathered from all the German yards, were concentrated in the small city of Blankenburg, situated in the Harz mountains, far away from any bombing menace. They formed the *Ingenieurbureau Glueckauf,* responsible for detail design and construction planning, and it was these men who provided the detail design for the new mass-produced U-boat. A full-scale wooden mock-up was built to study the boat's interior and decide on the ideal placing of the torpedo tubes, machinery and other features, under as near actual conditions as could be created. In August 1943 some suppliers received their first

orders, at the end of September the first steel consignments were available – through Speer's invaluable intervention – and in November the first 170 units were ordered.

PRODUCTION PROBLEMS
Three yards were chosen for the final assembly: Deschimag (Bremen), Blohm & Voss (Hamburg) and Schichau (Danzig). Each was ordered to build a prototype to gain experience for mass production of the final version. For prestige reasons the HAS wanted the three prototype units to be launched on Hitler's birthday, 19 April 1944, and, to keep to this schedule, some of the suppliers delivered half-finished sections which the main yards had to complete in addition to their final assembly work. Only Schichau was able to launch one of the vessels, *U3501*, on the required day, the other builders being unwilling to launch an incomplete boat. Even

The French *Roland Morillot*, ex *U2518*, was employed on extensive trials the results of which were utilised in the design of the *Narwal* class.

USN, courtesy A D Baker III

U3501 was far from being in true launching trim – all her openings were provisionally plated over with wood, the boat had to be drydocked immediately after launch, and she was not actually commissioned until 29 July 1944.

Of course, such a decisive programme imposed a heavy load on German industry in the fifth year of war: for example, it took 50 per cent of the capacity of all German iron-working facilities to produce the basic sections, and important other programmes had to be postponed. It was also found that the suppliers of the basic sections could not maintain the required fitting tolerances, so the assembling yards had to do additional work in order to get the various sections to fit together. The bombing of German industrial centres and transport routes also caused much delay in the delivery of such vital parts as electric motors, batteries and persicopes. Consequently, the optimistic production estimates could not be maintained, although all yards worked around the clock while Germany fell into ruins around them. After the collapse of the Weichsel front and the loss of Danzig, the two western yards continued production, but following the breakdown of internal German traffic in the Spring of 1945 (caused by Allied bombing) all construction work ceased and only repairs were carried out.

OPERATIONAL HISTORY

By 1 August 1944, one year after preliminary mass production had begun, 8 boats had been delivered to the Kriegsmarine – *U2501–2504*, *U3001*, *U3002*, *U3501* and *U3502*. They were employed as training boats but also served to obtain practical experience with the new type and for fault-finding and locating design errors. As the boats were very different from the old types in behaviour and abilities, a new attack scheme had to be worked out. Despite the catastrophic general situation in the Spring of 1945 the Germans assembled in the Baltic a number of target-practice convoys, including escorts, to train the first combat crews. Following the loss of Danzig, the boats already training in the Baltic returned to the west. During this transfer *U3007*, *U2506* and *U2519* passed the sinking KdF-liner

The second Type XXI to be tested by the US Navy, *U3008*, was fitted with a new streamlined conning tower to evaluate its hydrodynamic performance for future US submarine designs.

USN, courtesy A D Baker III

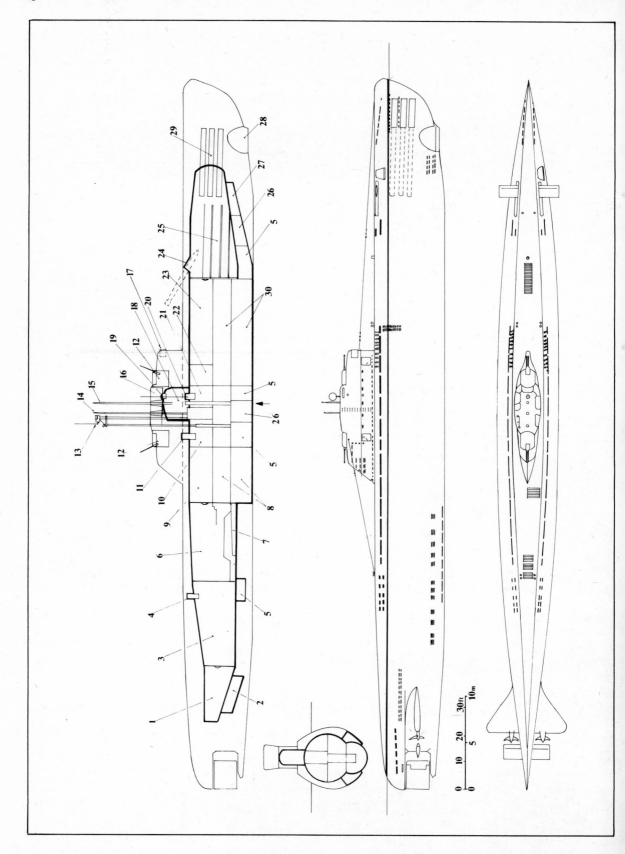

GENERAL ARRANGEMENT OF TYPE XXI SUBMARINE

KEY: **1** Stern compartment, auxiliary engines; **2** Trimming tank; **3** Motor room; **4** Motor room hatch; **5** Diving tank; **6** Diesel room; **7** Diesel engine seatings; **8** After battery compartments; **9** Crew space; **10** Galley; **11** Galley hatch; **12** Twin 2cm AA mounting; **13** Snorkel; **14** Attack periscope; **15** Air-search periscope; **16** Bridge; **17** Pinger transmitter; **18** Tower; **19** Tower hatch; **20** Central hatch; **21** Operations centre; **22** Captain's cabin; **23** Living space; **24** Torpedo loading hatch; **25** Torpedo compartment, spare torpedoes; **26** Regulating tank; **27** Trimming tank; **28** Sonar dome; **29** Torpedo tubes; **30** Forward battery compartment. Note: section is at conning tower as indicated by arrow.

All drawings by the author

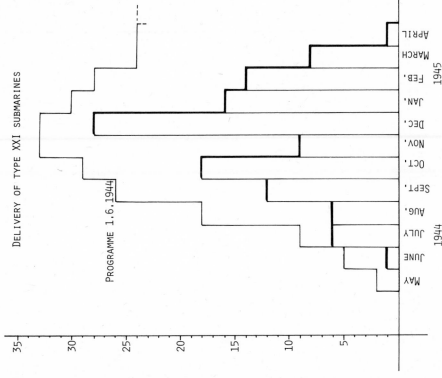

DELIVERY OF TYPE XXI SUBMARINES

PROGRAMME 1.6.1944

Wilhelm Gustloff (lost 30 January 1945; approximately 6000 dead) but were not allowed to stop and help for reasons of secrecy.

Most of the 'worked-up' boats were transferred to Norway to begin their first concentrated attack on Allied shipping. However, they were heavily attacked by the RAF in the Danish Belt, and nine boats were lost, so only two Type XXI boats, *U2511* and *U3008*, were actually available for the first operational mission.

U2511, under the command of *Korvettenkapitän* (Commander) Adalbert Schnee, was nicknamed 'The White Boat' because of the relation of snow (=*Schnee*) to the white colour. It was the only boat that was fully equipped with all the projected radar and sonar gear as the delivery of much of this equipment to the other commissioned boats was delayed by production shortages.

Schnee left Horten base on 30 April 1945 but, after reaching a position to the west of the Shetlands/Faeroes passage, Dönitz radioed a general cease-fire for all submarines. Schnee therefore broke off his mission and returned to base. During this return he encountered a British task force, penetrated its escort and made a training attack from 500m (550yds) on the cruiser *Norfolk*, without firing his torpedoes. Later, Schnee reported his attack to the astonished officers of *Norfolk*, when she lay in Horten with the British occupying forces.

Today Schnee runs a very successful sailing school at Portoferraio on the island of Elba.

U3008, under the command of *Kapitänleutnant* (Lieutenant-Commander) Helmut Manseck, left Wilhelmshaven on 3 May 1945. The boat was in the northern North Sea when the capitulation was radioed and, a short time later, Manseck met a British task force on its way to occupy Copenhagen. Ignoring a British order to go directly to Loch Eireboll, he returned to Frederikshaven and later to Kiel.

Of the completed boats, 121 units had been commissioned; 9 were sunk during the transfer to Norway, 2 were mined in the Baltic, 12 were bombed during fitting out, 86 were scuttled by their crews (3–5 May 1945, following Dönitz's famous 'rainbow-order') and 12 boats were delivered to the Allies.

POSTWAR FATES

After the German surrender the British found 28 boats nearing completion on the slips at Hamburg and Bremen, surrounded by dozens of prefabricated sections. They were surprised to learn that, despite all efforts to bomb out German shipyards and industry, their enemies were still capable of building and commissioning such a large number of new submarines. Most of the scuttled boats were raised and scrapped in 1945–47, while the surviving boats were distributed between the Allies under the terms of the Potsdam Conference, as follows:

U2502, *U2506* and *U2511* to Britain; scuttled in North Atlantic

during 'Operation Deadlight'.
U2513 to USA; employed in trials and sunk on 7 October 1951 as practice target off Key West after rocket hit.
U2518 to France, 1947; renamed *Roland Morillot,* experimental ship, condemned 17 October 1967.
U2529 to Britain as *N27*; ceded to USSR 1947.
U3008 to USA; employed in trials and broken up 1951.
U3017 to Britain as *N41*; broken up November 1949.
U3035 to Britain as *N28*; ceded to USSR 1947.
U3041 to Britain as *N29*; ceded to USSR 1947.
U3514 to Britain; scuttled in North Atlantic during 'Operation Deadlight'.
U3515 to Britain as *N30*; ceded to USSR 1947.

Postwar trials with the Type XXI submarines led to the US Navy's GUPPY programme (see *Warship 9*, page 38) and French experiments with the *Roland Morillot* had a strong influence on the design of the first six postwar French submarines of the *Narwal* class. Great Britain was more interested in the Walter propulsion system and kept no Type XXI submarines for trials.

Apart from the four Type XXI submarines ceded to the Soviets by Britain in 1947 it is not known how many almost complete boats fell into Soviet hands after the conquest of Danzig. It may be guessed that they assembled some boats from the mass of prefabricated sections available and that they completed the construction of some of the boats found on the slips. The first postwar Russian submarine type, the 'Whiskey' class, of which over 200 were built, show some features of their German ancestors.

The only surviving Type XXI is the former *U2540* which was scuttled on 4 May 1945 near the Flemsburg lightship . In 1957 she was raised, repaired and commissioned as *Wal* (whale) for the Federal German Navy and on 1 September 1960 was renamed *Wilhelm Bauer* (after the inventor of the first continental submarine *Brandtaucher*).

Several prefabricated sections for Type XXI submarines in the early stages of construction. All are No 7 sections (bow torpedo room), the only section to have a curved floor. The lower part of the double cylinder contained the pressure-proof trimming cells.

USN, courtesy A D Baker III

CONCLUSION

The German Type XXI submarine was not the 'miracle submarine' indicated by Hitler's propaganda. Its hull design and its abilities were a clear reaction to the demands of recent submarine warfare and new Allied ASW techniques. The weapons, ranging and detection systems were the next logical step to meet these new demands and were the initial move towards the electronic and fully automatic weapons systems in service today.

For the crews of the old boats, who had practically no chance of surviving the remorseless Allied anti-submarine campaign, the abilities of the new boats were of course 'fantastic' and 'miraculous'. Naturally, the rapid development and construction of the boats resulted in considerable problems and many imperfections. Some of the machinery proved over-sophisticated and badly constructed, while the fitting tolerances of the prefabricated sections were poor. In addition, at this stage of the war, Germany was seriously short of the high-quality material necessary for modern

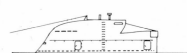

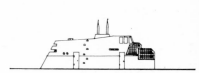

CONNING TOWER VARIATIONS IN POST WAR TYPE XXI SUBMARINES
From top to bottom: US *U2513*, US *U3008*, French *Roland Morillot* (ex *U2518*) and the West German *Wilhelm Bauer* (ex *U2540*)

manufacturing and had to use whatever substitutes were available; moreover, she did not have the required numbers of highly skilled workers to put it together. If there had been sufficient time to develop the type, under peacetime conditions, it is probable that none of these problems would have occurred. Even with the production shortcomings, the French Type XXI, *Roland Morillot*, attained the surprising service age of 23 years. A most profound statement regarding the potential of the type was made by Lt Cdr A N Glennon, the US Commander of *U3008*: 'Had the Germans been able to get the Type XXI to sea a year earlier, these submarines would probably have had a serious effect on our ability to keep our Allies supplied with the necessary materials of war.'

Part 2 of this article will cover the technical details of the Type XXI.

A close-up of the conning tower of a Type XXI submarine.

BfZ

The West German *Wilhelm Bauer*, former *U2540* scuttled in April 1945 and raised in 1957. Under the Contract of Paris of 1954 Federal German Navy submarines were limited to 350 tons standard displacement but for this vessel an exception was made with the provision that she be employed for trials and tests only. She was repaired and refitted by Howaltswerke at Kiel during 1958-60 under the name *Wal* but was renamed when commissioned on 1 September. She was completely modernised by Blohm and Voss at Hamburg during 1968-70 since when she has served as a trials and experimental ship for new equipment. She is manned by a civilian crew.

USN, courtesy A D Baker III

The Chester Class Cruisers

by Norman Friedman

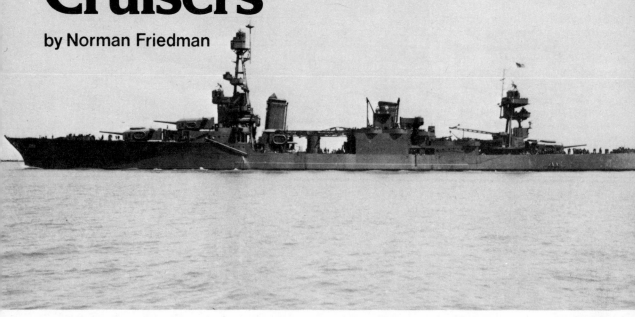

Of the 18 heavy cruisers the US Navy built under a succession of naval arms limitation treaties, the six *Chester*s, CA-26–31, were probably the most graceful. They also provide a fine illustration of a common American phenomenon in which quite considerable design changes occurred from class to class well before any sea-going experience had been obtained. American warship construction has usually been characterised by bursts of rapid activity following long periods of relative neglect. Thus, the basic design of each programme is influenced by experience with relatively elderly, often obsolete, types, while many of the later variations on the new theme reflect service dissatisfaction with the paper characteristics of the first design. That was the case with many of the '1500-ton' destroyers of the 1930s and, ten years earlier, it was very much the case in heavy cruiser design. The first of the new cruisers to be completed was *Salt Lake City*, commissioned on 11 December 1929. By that time not only the

*Chester*s and their successors the *Portland*s but also the *New Orleans* class has passed through design and has been laid down. The *New Orleans* represented very nearly a clean break with earlier ideas and even the *Chester*s showed considerable development as compared to the first pair of US 'treaty' cruisers.

A total of 6 cruisers was authorised under a December 1924 Cruiser Bill; the first funds covered the two *Salt Lake City* class units, three more were funded partially under the May 1926 Appropriation Bill and the remaining three under a March 1927 measure. After bids had been received for the first triplet, which became CA-23–28, it was decided to order all six (CA-26–31) as a group. The first three were built as division flagships, the last three (CA-29–31) as fleet flagships, with additional space for an Admiral's staff. They proved more useful in this role than did the subsequent *New Orleans* class, since, in the latter, accommodation space had to

be traded off against increased protection. Thus in 1939 *Houston* (CA-30) served as alternate flagship for the US Fleet; she later transferred to the Asiatic Fleet and was sunk as its flagship. *Augusta* (CA-31) held that position in 1939, and later became flagship of the Atlantic Fleet (1941). In 1939, too, *Chicago* was flagship of cruisers, Scouting Force. *Indianapolis* (CA-35), also designed as a flagship, was flagship of the entire Scouting Force. She might best be described as an improved *Chester,* with slightly better protection but still with considerable internal volume for flag accommodations.

ORIGINS

The *Chester*s had two separate origins. First, there was a feeling within the design organisation of the Bureau of Construction and Repair (C&R) that the *Salt Lake City* design sacrificed too much in order to mount the maximum battery of ten 8in guns. It was accepted that no great improvement in protection could be achieved but it did seem possible to improve the balance between firepower and sea-going characteristics. That is, the earlier design traded some hull weight for extra guns – a relatively shallow hull was adopted, while deep draught was required for good sea-going qualities. The consequence was limited freeboard, so, well before

these two ships were completed, C&R expected them to be wet amidships and even abreast their forward turrets. A related sacrifice was hull length, purchased in part by crowding eight boilers into two boiler rooms. To some extent, too, the aircraft arrangement of the two cruisers were not entirely satisfactory. For example, aircraft could not be protected from the blast of the main battery guns firing on extreme angles of bearing. Captain L B McBride, head of the Design Section, suspected that a far more satisfactory design could be obtained by the sacrifice of one or two guns, ie by adopting either a three-gunhouse type or by retaining the four gunhouses of the *Salt Lake*

City but reverting to all twin mounts, as in foreign designs.

The other, and the driving, impulse towards a new cruiser came from the General Board, responsible for the characteristics (staff requirements) for new warships. In 1926 funds for three new cruisers were in prospect and the Board sought improvements over the existing *Salt Lake City* design. About the middle of February 1926, one member of the Board, Admiral Wiley, asked C&R to investigate the consequences of providing two additional boiler room bulkheads, to break up the two large boiler rooms of the *Salt Lake City* design and so to restore a measure of survivability against

In June 1944, *Chester* still had much her prewar silhouette, with a high tripod forward and a stump mast aft. Her open bridge (numeral 3) had been fitted in a previous refit. Radars evident here are SK on the foremast, with Mk 3 below it, and SG (for surface search) on the lattice mast aft. Mk 4 still surmounts the Mk 33 5in directors.

USN

underwater attack. It should be noted here that such attack was, as yet, considered a far more serious threat to a large fast cruiser than was cruiser shellfire. For example, until the *Portland* class US cruisers had their magazines raised well above the inner bottom to protect them from underwater explosions. As it became evident that cruisers could actually achieve a fair percentage of hits at long range, pressure mounted to move the magazines below the waterline, an

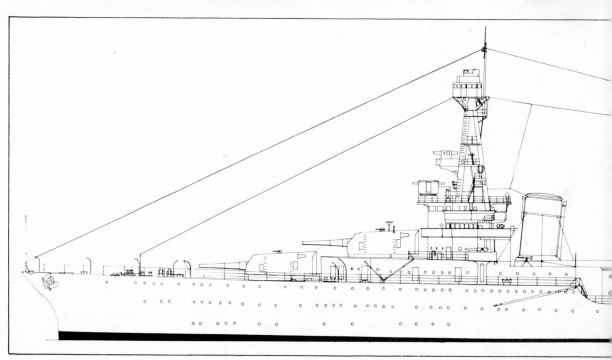

Three views of *Chester,* shown after her final refit at Mare Island on 13 May 1945. The circles show alterations, which included the removal of the rangefinder of No 1 turret, as weight compensation, and the installation of a forecastle quadruple Bofors as well as twin Oerlikons. Note, too, the open sight ports in No 1 turret and the new windshield protecting the open bridge. The new mainmast carried both the SP fighter-control radar and a complete ECM outfit: a TDY jammer on a topmast, DBM radar direction-finders on a lattice yard below it, intercept antennas flanking the mast below that and an S-band jammer in the large radome below them. The latticework platform built out from the mainmast was intended to carry a magnetic compass clear of most of the ship's steel. The yardarm, at SP level, carries, from left to right, an IFF antenna, TBS tactical radio and another IFF set.

USN

evolution in the design of the *New Orleans* (see *Warship 11*). Preliminary estimates showed an increase in length of 12–20ft and a cost in weight of about 160–200 tons. It was not yet suspected that careful weight-saving would bring in the first pair of Treaty cruisers at about a thousand tons under the 10,000-ton limit so this 160–200 tons seemed, in 1926, a considerable cost.

Captain McBride suggested a reduction to nine guns in three gunhouses as a weight-saver. The

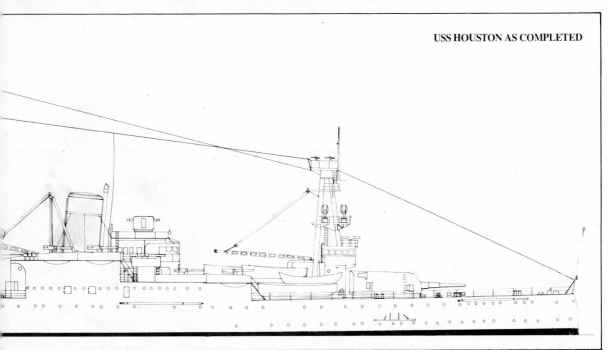

USS HOUSTON AS COMPLETED

Preliminary Design section looked towards an increase in hull depth, which could reduce stresses and permit the use of lighter hull scantlings. To some extent, too, the bending moment of the hull might be reduced by moving fuel oil tanks from the ends of the ship to amidships, outboard of the machinery spaces, 'in as much as the evaporating plant, being too long to stow in the short boiler rooms contemplated, would have to be placed outside the machinery spaces anyhow. It was thought that if the bending moment could be reduced sufficiently enough weight might be saved in scantlings to provide for a forecastle which was greatly desired both for the added freeboard it would secure and for the additional space it would provide for the accommodation of officers and crew.'

The General Board seemed willing to accept not only the reduced battery but also some reduction in armour as weight compensation; ultimately 0.25in had to be shaved from the already scanty side protection, to leave 3.75in and 3.25in respectively, over the fore and aft magazines, and 2.75in over the machinery spaces amidships. On deck, protection was limited to 1.5in over magazine and 1in over machinery. On the other hand, the increased freeboard (ie increased reserve buoyancy), increased degree of compartmentation and reduced clear width in machinery spaces all made for better resistance to underwater damage, ie to flooding. Later in the course of the design a weight saving of 200 tons would be applied to the ammunition hoists, increasing their protection from 0.75in to 1.5in. This still left the gunhouses at best weakly protected, with 2.5in face plates and 1.5in roofs.

A summary of the new design prepared in March 1926 shows an expected increase in speed of about 0.2kts as compared to the *Salt Lake City*, given the greater length of the ship. Any prospective loss in manoeuvrability would be made up for by cutting away more of the deadwood aft. Freeboard aft would increase by about 2ft but, owing to the adoption of the forecastle, abreast the fore turrets, forward superstructure and stack the improvements would be 5–8ft; 'this is believed a great improvement.'

ACCOMMODATION

There was considerable interest in habitability, a concern which seems sadly familiar to modern ears. Volume studies showed an increase per man of about 15 per cent compared to the *Salt Lake City* class. There was a general gain in volume, due to the forecastle, but volume assigned to machinery decreased, owing to the reduced width of the machinery spaces (due to oil storage amidships), and the elimination of one turret reduced ordnance volume. In 1926 the issue of bunks, rather than hammocks, for the crew had been under study for some years, and the *Chester*s were the first major US warships to be designed for bunks. Experimental installations had been fitted in the battleships *California* and *Oklahoma* but the two *Salt Lake City* class cruisers were designed without them 'as reports had not been received from the battleships. Destroyers and submarines are fitted with bunks and it is now proposed to extend their use to all classes of war vessels.' In approving this decision, Secretary of the Navy Long observed that '. . .there are no two things more conducive to contentment, and therefore to efficiency, than comfortable sleep and good food well served . . . The Department has approved the principle of the highest standards possible in these respects. Bunks provide the highest standard of sleeping conditions possible for the crew onboard ship. The petty annoyances that are inseparable from the use of hammocks do not attach to bunks . . . bunks should be provided for all the crew instead of for part of the crew . . .' Objections were raised that the bunks would encroach upon open spaces for recreation and assembly of the crew and for shelter in bad weather, as well as upon mess spaces. It was also suggested that bunks above the second deck would constitute a splinter hazard. An alternative scheme which overcame these problems, however, would have left 20 per cent of the crew in hammocks. It was rejected; messing arrangements were altered to utilise a large space previously reserved for a reading and recreation room: 'as mess tables are spread for but short periods three times a day, and as messing spaces for both officers and men are kept clean and neat as other compartments, this compartment can appropriately serve well the double purpose . . .'

The splinter issue was more serious and its resolution has a modern ring. The General Board commented that 'if shells enter they will, in all probability, explode before they get out whether bunks are there or not. If the crew is at battle stations as it will be in action, there will be but few if any people in these compartments anyway. It should be remembered that we shall probably be at war but a small percentage of the time which will constitute the life of these ships. When a war comes, if it is deemed advisable to remove bunks from No 2 deck, it can be easily and readily done and there will be no lowering of morale by so doing. In time of war officers and men expect discomfort, even hardship. They cheerfully accept it, and while appreciating such comfort as can properly be allowed, it is by the nature of things of secondary importance to them as compared to its importance in time of peace – our normal condition.' This issue of habitability versus military efficiency was to come up again and again in the prewar fleet and it has achieved great prominence in recent years. In peacetime it was not merely a matter of efficiency; the prewar US Navy was a volunteer force, traditionally troubled by high rates of desertion. It did not have nearly the same re-enlistment problem as it has today, but personnel comfort was not far from the centre of concern.

AIRCRAFT ARRANGEMENTS

Aircraft arrangements were another important issue. The US 10,000-ton

The newly completed USS *Augusta*, February 1931.
CPL

cruisers were expected to perform a variety of missions, including 'strategic' or independent scouting and commerce protection against surface raiders. In each case scout aircraft would be essential, and they would have to be carried in a hangar, protected against the blast of shellfire. In the 1920s the performance gap between wheeled (carrier) aircraft and floatplanes was not nearly as large as it would be a decade later and the new cruisers were intended to operate two floatplane fighters as well as two scout, or observation, aircraft. Enough hangar space was ultimately provided for them to accommodate eight aircraft with wings folded, and the catapults could launch the then considerable weight of 6500lb.

The hangar and catapults shifted back and forth during the design of the ships. A sketch plan prepared late in March 1926 shows the hangar quite far aft, just forward of No 3 turret, with catapults between it and the after funnel, and a light pole mainmast – an arrangement similar to that later adopted for the *New Orleans* class. Cranes were to be stepped abreast the second funnel, to serve both boats and aircraft; the aircraft were to be moved from hangar to catapults on trolleys so that an additional crane, serving the hangar proper, was not required.

Captain McBride moved the hangar forward to surround the after uptakes, and in the process

The *Chester,* as refitted, shows the characteristic frame of the first US air-search radar, CXAM, at her foretop. In this 1942 photograph she shows a mixed light battery of quadruple 1.1in machine cannon and 20mm Oerlikons.

USN

The *Chester*, as refitted at Mare Island, on 16
September 1943 shows her new open bridge,
without bridge wings to interfere with the sky
arcs of the quadruple 40mm mounted at the
01 level below and abaft it. The former
main-battery rangefinder had been
eliminated in favour of additional Oerlikons,
and all her radars are visible: SG
surface-search sets fore and aft, SK air-search,
Mk 3 for the main battery, Mk 4 for her
secondaries, Also notable is the sharp
reduction in searchlights as compared to
1942: battle experience in the Solomons
showed that they were a definite and severe
hazard in night actions. The objects just
visible on the 01 level, outboard of No 2
turret, are the floats of a floater net, another
consequence of the lessons of the disastrous
Solomons cruiser/destroyer night actions.

USN

This amidships detail view, taken on 10 April 1945, shows the ventilator which replaced the starboard catapult. Note, too, the 20mm gun, circled at left, with the four helmets of its crew hanging from the shield. The two objects circled at the foretop (below the SG radar) are NANCY infra-red beacons and the Mk 13 main battery fire control radar, which was then replacing the comb-like Mk 8.

USN

achieved considerable economy. A single crane stepped from a small tripod forward of this funnel could handle both aircraft and boats but, on the other hand, it might not extend far enough over the side to recover aircraft from the water. The ingenious solution was a hoist mounted directly on the underside of the catapult proper so that the catapult could be turned to bring an aircraft on board, landing it on the extensive well deck between forecastle and hangar. The mainmast proper remained aft, a stub tripod surrounded by fire controls.

SECONDARY ARMAMENT

The secondary battery was subject to considerable change. Originally it was intended that the ships be armed with a 37mm automatic cannon which was under development. Two pairs of 5in/51 starshell guns were to be mounted on the forecastle. Apparently it was expected that the 8in main battery would suffice to break up destroyer torpedo attacks. In fact the 37mm gun did not materialise in time and 5in/25 AA guns had to be substituted and, as these could also fire starshell, they replaced the 5in/51s. As early as August 1932 the Bureau of Ordnance suggested that the secondary battery be doubled; the basic issue was the purpose of the 5in guns. BuOrd maintained that the slow-firing 8in weapons were entirely unsuited to anti-destroyer fire, in view of their rate of fire, the type of mounting employed (with all three guns in one sleeve) and the limited ammunition supply (150 rounds per 8in gun). In February 1933 the General Board approved the addition of four more 5in/25 guns to achieve a broadside of at least four guns for defence against

destroyers; at this time BuOrd also wanted a heavier AA barrage. The new policy also called for the installation of AA directors (Mk 19), and in the same year the installation of eight 0.50in machine guns was approved. The progress of this programme was symptomatic of the funding of the prewar US Navy: although the Chief of Naval Operations agreed to it on 25 February, and the Secretary of the Navy agreed at about the same time, it was not until February 1935 that a programme was undertaken. Even then funds were assigned only for FY39 (ie, the year beginning 1 July 1938, for preliminary fittings for CA-28–30; FY40, for completion of CA-28–30 and

preliminary work and installations for CA-26 and 27; and FY41, for CA-31.

ARMOUR

As for protection, the ships were the victims of a radical shift in perceptions of the threat, from destroyer to cruiser fire. They were not designed to any particular standard of immune zone; that measure of protection was not adopted until the *New Orleans* was designed in about 1929. However, a 1933 navy study showed that they would be proof against 5.1in (destroyer) fire outside 7000yds (magazines; 8000 for machinery). Against 6in/50 fire, however, they would be limited to a band between

10,000 and 21,000yds (magazines); the belt over their machinery would resist such fire beyond 13,000yds but on the other hand the deck over machinery would be penetrable at that range. Worse still, there would be no immunity at all against 8in/50 fire. The belt over the magazines could be penetrated at 21,000 and the deck at 20,000yds, and the belt over machinery was vulnerable at 24,000 and the deck at 13,000yds.

The lack of protection became a matter of concern almost as soon as the contract design was complete. A C&R memorandum of February 1927 shows what would have been required to protect the magazine and machinery spaces against 8in fire. A drastic reduction in the estimated design margin (ie, a calculated risk that the ships, as completed, would exceed the Treaty Limit), the reduction of gunhouse armour to blast shielding, and considerable decreases in magazine volume (ie, in rate of fire) and in some side plating would buy 7in side armour over magazines, 4in over the vital gunnery 'central' (plotting and computing station) and 3.5in over the machinery spaces. Deck protection would increase to 2in over magazines and machinery. The reduction in gunhouse armour was not very drastic, given the light plating available in any case, but it did save 113 tons; the margin amounted to 215 tons. As a more balanced alternative, C&R considered protecting the guns against the risk of disability through 6in splinters below deck, or 6in direct hits above, trying at the same time to improve magazine protection. This would require 4in faceplates and 2in crowns for the gunhouses. Magazines would shrink, and their sides would be thickened to 7in. In effect, the last two ships of the *Chester* series, the two *Portland*s, did trade much of the constructional margins actually achieved in the former for increased side armour, 5.75in over magazines and 3in over machinery. As for the *Chester*s, none of the drastic proposals was approved, the General Board agreeing in the end to no more than the 0.75in increase in ammunition hoist protection already described.

ALTERNATIVE DESIGNS

Quite early in the design process an alternative four-gunhouse, eight-gun design was considered, a configuration traditionally favoured, and actually adopted by other Treaty-cruiser navies. Given the unsatisfactory character of the four-turret *Salt Lake City*, it was suspected from the outset that three turrets would be better and that proved correct – from a design point of view. This choice was in fact symptomatic of the American process of design evolution. In other navies, the choice of four turrets was most often justified on gunnery grounds, in terms of salvo size and spacing. The US Navy, however, had had no experience whatever with a three-turret ship when the *Chester* was designed, nor is it clear to what extent the gunnery sacrifices involved in their gun mount design had been considered. That is, the three-turret cruiser was made possible, to some extent, by the adoption of a gun mount with all of its weapons elevating together in a single unit. Since there was no sea-going experience with 8in gun cruisers in 1926, issues of weight, hull strength, internal arrangement and balance, between battery and protection, predominated.

In describing a tentative four-turret design, Preliminary Design wrote that 'in order not to crowd the end turrets too far towards the end of the ship it has been necessary to raise turrets Nos 2 and 3 high enough so that their overhangs may swing over the tops of Nos 1 and 4. It results that the common centre of gravity of the main battery in the 4-turret scheme is about 2½ft higher than in the 3-turret scheme. Also, in order to mount the high turrets, it has been necessary to provide additional superstructure . . . such changes would raise the centre of gravity of the ship between 0.3 and 0.4ft higher than that of the three-turret ship. It would then be necessary to increase the beam and decrease the draught, keeping the depth unchanged. The increase in weight involved would be some 40 to 50 tons, principally in bulkheads, decks, shell plating, etc . . . but partly also in an increased width of

side belt to maintain its depth below normal water line at 5ft . . . it will be necessary to cut the thickness of the side belt below that of the nine-gun ship by about 7 to 10 pounds' ie by up to another 0.25in.

WAR MODIFICATIONS

The progression of war modification was typical of the US prewar-built cruiser force. In 1940 the King Board recommended urgent improvements in AA fire power, ultimately to provide four quadruple 1.1in machine guns per cruiser. As these weapons were in short supply, 3in/50 guns would be provided as an interim battery, one per quadruple 1.1in. By this time the four extra 5in/25s had been mounted and the pair of triple 21in torpedo tubes originally mounted had been landed. The King Board also proposed extensive splinter protection for bridge and fire-control personnel and for the AA battery. As of December 1942, *Chester, Louisville, Chicago* and *Houston* had 3in guns, and *Augusta* had all her 1.1in, but it is not clear whether *Northampton* had either. Large Mk 19 directors in shields were fitted above the forebridge and atop the after fire controls. They were replaced by the newer Mk 33, originally intended for destroyer installation, in 1943–44 but *Houston* and *Northampton* were lost in 1942 while still carrying their Mk 19s. The main fire-controls were Mk 24s, with positions in the foretop and at the base of the stub mainmast aft.

By late 1941 the 40mm Bofors gun and the 20mm Oerlikon had been adopted as standard in place, respectively, of the 1.1in and the 0.5in machine gun. Ultimate AA plans showed four quadruple Bofors replacing the earlier quadruple 1.1in, the heavy cruisers having sufficient reserve stability to accept the additional weight; in lesser ships one twin Bofors equated to a quad 1.1in. First, however, quadruple 1.1in were fitted in place of the 3in/50s still installed in many cases; thus in August 1942 *Chester* emerged from a refit with no 3in guns, two quadruple 1.1in and 13–20mm.

By mid-1942 BuShips planned drastic changes in superstructure to enlarge AA arcs of fire. Bridge wings were to be cut back and open upper bridges fitted. These alterations applied to virtually every class of warship. In the *Chester* class there was also a later modification to save top weight – a reduction of the foremast to the level of the secondary conning position, formerly half way up that mast, the resulting stub tripod being braced externally. It would then roughly match the cut-down foremast actually fitted to *Portland* and *Indianapolis* as built. The stub mainmast, carrying both 8in and 5in controls, was not affected. These alterations occurred in stages. Thus at least *Chester* and *Chicago* received the new bridge structure in the course of refits in, respectively, the Autumn of 1942 and the Spring of 1943. *Augusta* was probably similarly altered during a refit at New York Navy Yard between December 1942 and January 1943. *Augusta* operated for a time with her foremast cut down after a modernisation (November 1943 – April 1944) but the other two surviving units, *Chester* and *Louisville,* appear to have combined this alteration with the elimination of the stub mainmast.

War refits included both greatly increased light batteries and internal improvements to increase survivability. For example, the *Chester*s were built without emergency diesel generators, relying instead on storage batteries. During her refit at Norfolk (26 January – 30 July 1943) *Chester* was fitted with a single 100kW diesel, the type normally fitted to a destroyer but still a great advance for her. Two 400 gallons per minute fire pumps were mounted in her hold, as a result of lessons learned in the South Pacific campaign which had already claimed two of her sisters, *Chicago* and *Northampton*. She also received four quadruple and two twin Bofors guns, as well as 18 Oerlikons. Two of the quadruple 40mm were mounted on the 01 level abreast of the forward superstructure and two aft, just forward of the stub tripod, which in this refit was fitted for SG surface search radar. The two twin mounts were right aft, on the fantail, a feature not present in the *Chicago* just before her loss; it reflected the explosive growth of light batteries in wartime.

The final stage of reconstruction involved the elimination of the stub mainmast. The former main battery directors were replaced by modern Mk 34s with Mk 8 radar, as in the new cruisers; this improvement could not be extended to the *New Orleans* class in view of their limited weight and stability margins. One director (with its armoured barbette) was mounted atop the shortened fore tripod, another abaft the after funnel, with the after Mk 33 dual-purpose director mounted at about the location of the former mainmast, but at the level of the top of the hangar. The deck was extended well aft, nearly to No 3 gunhouse, to serve as a base for 20mm guns. By late 1943 a battery of four quadruple and four twin Bofors (including two at weather deck level abreast the after director) and 27 Oerlikons was envisaged. Thus in the Spring of 1945 *Louisville* was refitted: she lost her starboard catapult and the rangefinder of No 1 turret as weight compensation to gain a quadruple Bofors on the forecastle (centreline) and 13 twin Oerlikons in place of the former 25 single mounts. In addition she had four twin Bofors guns. The forecastle mount was intended to permit her to keep an aircraft crossing her bows under fire, a consideration of increasing importance as the Fleet came under Kamikaze attack late in 1944. Kamikaze warfare also required additional fire controls so that, ultimately, the nine 40mm mounts were controlled by four Mk 63 radar (blind-fire) directors as well as five Mk 51s. The new directors added to the power load to the extent that *Louisville* and other old heavy cruisers were considered power-critical by August 1944.

Chester was similarly refitted, in line with a general policy to provide the older cruisers with bow Bofors, and to gain weight compensation by replacing single with twin 20mm mounts. *Augusta*, still in the Atlantic, never received the fifth quadruple mount and carried 20 single 20mm at the end of the war.

These heavy cruisers were among the first US warships to be fitted with air search radars. Thus, of the first six sets produced (CXAM), four went into the heavy cruisers *Pensacola, Northampton, Chester* and *Chicago*. The antenna was generally on the foremast but *Chicago* carried hers (at least at first) atop a mainmast cleared of its usual complement of light automatic weapons. By early 1942 *Augusta* had the modified CXAM-1, and by mid-1943 all surviving units had the familiar SK 'mattress' on their foremasts, with SG surface search antennas fore and aft. By that time there was a requirement for an SP fighter-control set, to be mounted on the foremast, SK moving aft. In fact SP was mounted only in 1945, and then only in the two Pacific Fleet units, *Louisville* and *Chester*; it went atop the mainmast, with

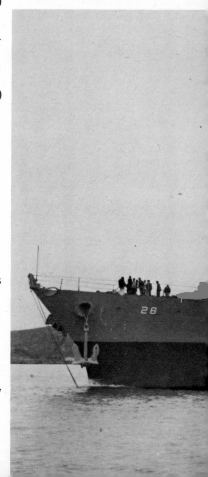

countermeasures gear (a TDY jammer and DBM radar direction-finders) below it. Again, these radar suits were typical of the US cruiser force at the time; SP often performed much the same role as the British target-indication sets, allowing a particular target to be tracked while the main search sets sought others.

All three ships were considered obsolete by 1946 and were placed on the disposal list. However, in 1952 they were restored to the Atlantic Reserve Fleet, from which they were stricken in 1959. Although modernisation plans were drawn up as part of the general compilation of Class Improvement Plans in 1952, it does not appear that reactivation or conversion for alternative service was ever seriously proposed. Among other things, weight growth in wartime had been considerable. For example, as completed *Chester* displaced 8510 tons in Condition II, ie with no fuel or other disposable weights on board (Navy Light

condition); she was rated at 12,851 tons fully loaded. In 1940, her light displacement had risen to 9107 tons, and she came to 13,533 tons fully loaded, with eight 5in/25 aboard. BuShips tried to control weight growth in wartime, and even with a very heavy AA battery she displaced only 9264 tons light (13,905 tons fully loaded) in July 1943. Similarly, *Louisville*, 8670 tons light as built (12,885 fully loaded), emerged twelve years later in 1945 almost a thousand tons heavier, at 9361 tons light and 14,030 fully loaded.

SOURCES

Basic design history is taken from the Preliminary Design file on these ships at the Federal Records Center, Suitland; material on the contract design (particularly aircraft arrangements and secondary battery) is from the design history in the Flat File on this class in the C&R records at the National Archives. The history of wartime alterations is taken from a variety of sources: the wartime correspondence files of the Bureau of Ships; wartime BuOrd Armament Summaries; records of the Ship Characteristics Board held by the Operational Archives; and the Inclining Experiment data compiled each time a major warship was refitted.

Off Mare Island on 7 April 1945, *Louisville* shows the final configuration of the class, with a short tripod foremast and a tall lattice mainmast carrying the SP fighter control radar. Modern Mk 34 main-battery directors and dual-purpose directors carry the Mk 28 radar, have been installed fore and aft. In ships with the later Mk 37 director, a combination of Mk 12 and the 'orange peel' Mk 22 was frequently fitted but these Mk 33s could not take that weight. Note, too, the forecastle quadruple 40mm mounting, to follow aircraft crossing the bows. The elimination of the starboard catapult (as weight compensation) is not evident here. *USN*

The Modified Leander Class

by Alan Payne MRINA

In the 1930s three new cruiser classes were designed to replace the old 'C' and 'D' class light cruisers of the 1913–18 War. The first two were the five *Leander* class and the three *Amphion*, or 'Modified Leander' class; the third class, consisting of smaller vessels with a lighter armament, were the four *Arethusa*s. At different stages before the outbreak of war in 1939, all three *Amphion*s were transferred to the Royal Australian Navy.

There can be little doubt that the 'Modified Leander' class were among the finest of the small cruisers built before the war. Although they were not the most heavily armed or the fastest, for a balanced design with superb machinery they had no equal in the world. The German light cruisers were armed with nine 5.9in guns in three turrets, two of which were aft, which meant that if the forward turret was hit not only one-third of the firepower but also all firepower forward would be lost. The Italian 'Condottieri' type were considerably lighter in displacement and sacrificed armour for speed but the high speeds obtained on trials bore no resemblance to their service speeds, hence *Bartolomeo Colleoni* was caught and sunk by HMAS *Sydney*, the first of the *Amphion*s.

The three new British light cruiser classes were the first to be affected by the London Naval Treaty of 1930, which limited the total tonnage of 6in cruisers allowed. They were also the first to be designed with 6in turrets, first tried in the cruiser *Enterprise* and also fitted in the new battleships *Nelson* and *Rodney*. The *Amphion*s were direct successors of the 'E' class cruisers, designed during the First World War, particularly as regards the unusual layout of the machinery spaces. The complete separation, into two widely spaced groups, of the engine rooms and boiler rooms was a very important feature of the 'E' class. In those ships bulge protection, of the type fitted in the much heavier *Raleigh* class cruisers, could only be provided at the expense of speed, unless the horsepower was considerably increased, and it was considered that the advantages gained by the separation of the machinery compartments would be equivalent to those obtained by a modified type of bulge. Particulars of the 'E' class and the *Amphion* class are given in Table 1.

The three cruisers of the *Amphion* class were laid down in 1933 and were allotted the names *Amphion*, *Phaeton* and *Apollo*. The

HMAS *Perth*, possibly taken at Alexandria, prior to her refit of January-February 1941. Her camouflage scheme is three colours – probably 507C, 507A and white – and she carries the aerials of radar Type 286 at the head of her maintopmast. Note the rangefinder baffles on her funnels.

Courtesy of the Author

first to be handed over to the Royal Australian Navy was *Phaeton*, which was transferred while still on the stocks and renamed *Sydney*. The second was *Apollo* which, after a short period with the Royal Navy, was transferred in January 1936 and renamed *Hobart*. Finally, the last member of the class was transferred in July 1939 and renamed *Perth*. Although all three cruisers distinguished themselves in action, the changes of name brough them ill luck and both *Sydney* and *Perth* were sunk, the former with all hands and the latter with very heavy casualties. *Hobart* was torpedoed in the Pacific but survived and was later considerably modified.

DISPLACEMENTS

It should be emphasised that the displacements of warships vary considerably with time, and even quoted figures are sometimes inaccurate when a ship is completed. In the Navy List, *Emerald* and *Enterprise* were rated

TABLE 1: PARTICULARS OF 'E' CLASS AND AMPHION CLASS (AS DESIGNED)

	'E' Class	Amphion
Length (oa)	570ft	562ft 3in
Length (pp)	535ft	530ft
Beam	54ft 6in	56ft 8in
Depth	31ft	32ft
Displacement (standard)	6900 tons	7105 tons
Displacement (deep)	8600 tons	9100 tons
Armament	7–6in guns	8–6in guns
	3–4in HA guns	8–4in HA guns
	16–21in torpedo tubes	8–21in torpedo tubes
Shp	80,000	72,000
Speed	33kts	32½kts
Endurance	–	8,800 miles at 20kts with cruising turbines in operation

TABLE 2: 'E' CLASS AND HOBART – WEIGHTS (tons)

	'E' Class (As designed)	Hobart (As built)
Equipment	360	490
Armament	355	690
Machinery	1590	1475
Armour and protective plating	700	880
Hull and fittings	3895	3570
Displacement (standard)	6900	7105

at 7550 tons, but this was actually their designed load displacement and included 650 tons of fuel. The standard displacements of the three Australian cruisers were given as 6830 tons for *Sydney*, 7105 for *Hobart* and 6908 for *Perth*. As the three ships were sisters these figures cannot be taken as being very accurate, and the big difference between *Sydney* and *Hobart* is probably due to the former not being fitted with a catapult and aircraft at the time and the latter having both catapult and aircraft in addition to twin 4in guns. In wartime, with various alterations and additions, the displacement increased considerably and in the case of *Hobart* the standard displacement in 1944 had increased from 7105 to 8040 tons. The best way of comparing two warships is by weights, and those for the 'E' class and *Hobart* are given in Table 2.

From Table 2 it will be noted that the two classes had very much the same displacement and, as might be

HMAS *Sydney,* shortly after completion, in October 1935. She retained her single 4in AA guns until lost, while both her sisters were refitted with twin 4in AA prior to the outbreak of war.

Wright and Logan

The *Hobart* after her 1943-45 refit. Her twin 4in guns have been re-positioned, abreast the forward funnel and after superstructure, and the close-range AA armament modified to: two 4 barrel Mk VII pom-poms, mounted on the former catapult support between the funnels; five single 40mm Mk IIIA Bofors mountings, two forward of the bridge, two abreast the after shelter deck and one on 'X' turret roof; three twin Mk IV Bofors mountings, two abreast the bridge structure and one on the quarterdeck; two single 20mm on the forward shelter deck; and one twin 20mm on the after control position. Her radar outfit consists of air-warning Type 281B (aerials at maintopmast head), surface warning Type 276 and US Type SG1 (aerials on foretopmast platform), air and surface warning Type 277 (aerial on foremast platform), main fire-control US Type FC1 (aerial on front of main DCT), two AA fire control type 285 (aerials on twin 40mm mountings and pom pom directors) and three AA barrage control Type 283 (aerials on barrage directors).

Courtesy of the author

The *Perth* during 1940 shows few modifications from her pre-war appearance. Carley rafts have been fitted and frames, for canvas rangefinder baffles, added to her funnels.

expected, the latter class had a much heavier armament weight owing to their twin 6in gun turrets compared with the single open mounts of the earlier ships. The weight of armour and protective plating was also increased and arranged more effectively. In the 'E' class the side protection extended from the stem to near the rudder head, following that previously adopted for light cruisers. In the *Hobart* and class the armour was mainly confined to protecting the machinery spaces; there was no point in attempting to protect the area forward when better use could be made of the available armour weight in protecting the most vital spaces.

The 'E' class had light, destroyer-type machinery of 80,000shp, while the *Hobart* and class had cruiser-type machinery of 72,000shp, so the reduction in weight of 115 tons does not represent the true position. A far better comparison would be with the 60,000shp machinery of the cruiser *Raleigh*, which weighed 1950 tons. It is evident that over the years there had been a vast improvement in marine engine and boiler design.

MACHINERY

As previously stated the machinery of the new cruisers was superb, and to this was added all the advantages of the 'unit system', allied to the spacing of the engine and boiler rooms. The 'unit system', first used by the British in the 'County' class 10,000-ton cruisers, is a matter of completely separate machinery systems – fuel, feed water, and live and exhaust steam. By cross-connecting valves, all systems can be interconnected for peacetime steaming or for emergency conditions. Any damage to one unit is thus completely isolated from the

other units. If 'de-united' prematurely, a ship can be in serious trouble if hit in the machinery spaces. This happened to the carrier *Ark Royal* when she was torpedoed on her way to Gibraltar for boiler cleaning in 1941. A major cause of this disaster was poor damage control – and the 'unit system' is, of course, a form of damage control.

The *Leander* class differed mainly from the 'improved *Leanders*' in that they did not have the spaced boiler and engine rooms and consequently had one large funnel while the new class had two funnels. Both classes were quadruple screw with 72,000shp, and both had four Admiralty 3-drum boilers with a designed speed of 32½kts. The design of the machinery reflects great credit on the Engineer-in-Chief's Department at the Admiralty. The big reduction in fuel consumption in *Sydney* was due to vastly improved turbine and boiler designs employing increased boiler pressures and superheated steam. Cruising turbines were fitted for greater economy at passage speeds up to about 22kts, and this saved about a ton of fuel an hour. At 20kts the fuel consumption was only 3½ tons per hour. On trials *Hobart* exceeded her design speed slightly, reaching 32.8kts at 72,550shp on a displacement of 7500 tons; at deep draught she reached 31.9kts. No effort seems to have been made to push the three cruisers much beyond their designed horsepower. As they put on weight during the war, their maximum speeds would, naturally, have fallen slightly.

Several British warships were lost during the war because they had no diesel generators, an extraordinary omission since all passenger ships had to have them by law. In the case of the *Sydney*s, this omission was rectified and, besides two 300kW steam generators (one in each engine room) they carried two diesel generators outside the machinery spaces, which were a great boon in harbour. At 'action stations' all four generators were always on line, with the ring main split for damage control purposes. When *Hobart* was torpedoed in the

Pacific the diesel generators were started up and connected in about two minutes.

PROTECTION
It is doubtful if any light cruisers of equal size to those of the *Sydney* class had better protection. The actual weights were 553 tons of armour and 329 tons of protective plating. Side armour 3in thick was fitted in way of the machinery spaces and, except abreast the after engine room, was carried up to the upper deck. Two-inch deck armour was fitted over the machinery spaces.

Perhaps the greatest compliment paid to the *Sydney* design was that the Germans copied it for six light cruisers which they laid down during the war but later scrapped on the stocks as it was obvious that they would not be ready in time. True, they were faster ships and slightly heavier, but otherwise they had the same arrangement of machinery and main armament. However, the Germans do not appear to have considered the 'unit system' for their ships, and, as usual, they went in for three shafts and very high pressure boilers, which gave them endless trouble.

WAR SERVICE
Under the command of Captain John Collins, RAN, HMAS *Sydney* sank the Italian light cruiser *Bartolomeo Colleoni* in the Mediterranean on 19 July 1940. This action emulated the duel between the previous *Sydney* and the German raider *Emden* in 1914. *Sydney* did not, unfortunately, survive the war, being lost with all hands in an action with the German raider *Kormoran* in the Indian Ocean on 19 November 1941, an engagement in which the raider was also sunk. *Sydney* was thus responsible for the greatest triumph of the Royal Australian Navy and also for its greatest tragedy.

HMAS *Perth* and USS *Houston* fought a most gallant action against a large Japanese fleet on 1 March 1942 in the Battle of Sunda Strait. Both Allied warships were sunk with heavy casualties and all survivors were taken prisoner. *Perth*

was under the command of Captain H M L Waller, DSO, RAN, who went down with his ship.

The third cruiser, *Hobart*, survived the war but was torpedoed in the Pacific on 21 July 1943. The cruiser was hit in the stern so casualties were light, four officers and three ratings being killed. After temporary repairs in the US naval base at Espiritu Santo *Hobart* returned to Sydney for permanent repairs and modernisation. The refit was not completed for 17 months, due to her being given a very low priority, and the cruiser did not recommission until 7 December 1944. During this refit tripod masts replaced the pole masts; the catapult structure was removed (the catapult and aircraft had been removed in 1941); more modern radar was fitted; the close range AA armament was greatly increased; and the 4in HA guns were resited a deck lower to improve stability.

In November 1943 the Admiralty sent a signal to the Australian and New Zealand authorities regarding cruiser armament: 'It has been decided to increase AA armament by surrendering 'X' turret in all four-turret cruisers and 'Q' in five-turret Didos.' The Australian Naval Board protested strongly that the stability of the *Hobart* was satisfactory and pointed out that, if 'X' turret was retained, space and weight would be available for two twin Oerlikons, three twin Bofors and two four-barrelled pompoms. The Admiralty promptly replied that, according to a 1942 inclining, the cruiser's stability in the light condition would not allow for any increased topweight. To this the Naval Board replied that the inclining experiment referred to had actually been based on the *Perth*. The signal stated: '*Hobart* inclined subsequently and revealed improved stability in light condition. Light condition, not including ammunition and with 175 tons of ballast, was 7336 tons, GM 1.86ft.' The signal then went on to give a detailed list of topweight surrendered, which included about 40 tons of wood deck and corticene and the lowering of boats one deck. It is interesting to note that on completion *Perth*'s GM in the light condition was 2.9ft, but before delivery to Australia this had been reduced to 2.2ft due to additional topweight. The GM in the average fighting, or half-oil, condition in the case of *Perth* was 4.0ft in 1936, 3.4ft in 1939 and 2.7ft in December 1941. *Hobart*'s GM would have been much the same.

In the end 'X' turret was retained for the war period and also the torpedo tubes. In March 1945 *Hobart*'s captain reported that the deep displacement was 9900 tons so, if this figure was exact, the deep displacement had been very slightly reduced as it was estimated to be 9908 in 1942. The maximum speed obtained in recent trials off Sydney was 31.5kts, but it is not known at what displacement the trials were run. The close-range armament fitted consisted of two four-barrelled pompoms, five single 40mm Bofors, three twin 40mm Bofors, two single 20mm Oerlikons and one twin Oerlikon. The gunnery statement gives the maximum range of the 6in guns as 24,800yds and that of the 21in torpedoes as 10,000yds at 40kts and 14,000yds at 35kts.

Between May and September 1946, *Hobart* was under refit, and it was finally decided to remove 'X' turret, but in August 1947 she was paid off into reserve. The next 15 years of her life is a sad story of unfulfilled decisions and plans during which extensive refits and modernisation were commenced but never completed. In September 1952 a decision was finally made to convert *Hobart* to a training ship, and she was towed to Newcastle, NSW, for this purpose; however, the contract was later cancelled. In February 1960 it was finally decided to scrap the cruiser, and in February 1962 she was sold to the Miyachi Shipyard, Osaka, and arrived in Japan on 2 April.

The term 'return to sanity' in cruiser construction was applied to the 8in-gun cruisers *Exeter* and *York*, which were about 1750 tons below the 10,000-ton limit, the maximum allowed by the Washington Treaty. The term could have been used far more accurately

for the *Leander*s and the 'Modified *Leander*s. The *Leander*'s were criticised for being too costly, but this was not fair comment as the cost of warship construction had risen sharply since the war. All eight cruisers of the two classes served with distinction during the Second World War.

1 The *Apollo* as completed, on 21 October 1935. She and *Amphion* were transferred to the RAN in 1938 and 1939 respectively and renamed *Perth* and *Hobart*.
CPL

2 The *Perth* in July 1939 departing Portsmouth, after refit, for Australia. Her single 4in have been replaced by twin Mk XIX 4in mountings but, unlike *Hobart*, she did not receive the intended aircraft catapult.

Wright and Logan

VERSUCHSGLEITBOOT
the world's first hovercraft

by Franz Ferdinand Bilzer

1 The 'Versuchsgleitboot' on the slip. The original 45cm torpedoes, in their troughs, and the hovering fan casing are clearly visible.

2 The 'Versuchsgleitboot' running at 27kts.

The practical development of the idea of reducing the hydrodynamic resistance of a vessel by blowing air under the hull dates back to the first years of this century.

Lieutenant-Commander (*Linienschiffsleutnant*) Dagobert Müller von Thomamuehl, of the Austro-Hungarian Navy first made intensive studies of this problem when he was commander of torpedo-boat *60T* (ex-*Schwalbe*). His idea was to reduce both resistance and displacement by lifting the hull out of the water on a cushion of pressurised air. He made model-towing tests, on his own initiative, using the torpedo-boat he commanded, and his knowledge of the science of testing scaled-down models was so great that all his figures and diagrams show an astonishing engineering brillance.

THE FIRST DESIGN

On 26 March 1915 he submitted to the Austrian Naval Technical Committee (*Marinetechnisches Komitee*, MTK) a paper entitled 'Study on the construction of a high-speed gliding boat'. The accompanying drawing showed a rectangular boat with hull dimensions of 16.3 x 6.6 x 0.75m (53.3 x 20.9 x 1.8ft) and a displacement 12.25 tonnes (12.05 tons). This was a true hovercraft employing two (or three, depending on the engines available) Austrodaimler aircraft engines of 120hp each for surface propulsion, and one 65hp Austrodaimler engine, driving an aircompressor giving 450m³ of air per minute (15,734 cu ft per min) for hovering. The vessel was designed for a speed of 32kts an endurance of 550nm and an armament of 4—45cm torpedoes in outboard containers.

When looking at this first design, one notes some very important features of hovercraft design. The fan was situated in the forward section of the rectangular hull and produced an air cushion over the full length of the bottom, allowing the boat to rise nearly 10in. Skirts at both sides prevented the air from escaping but there were no skirts at

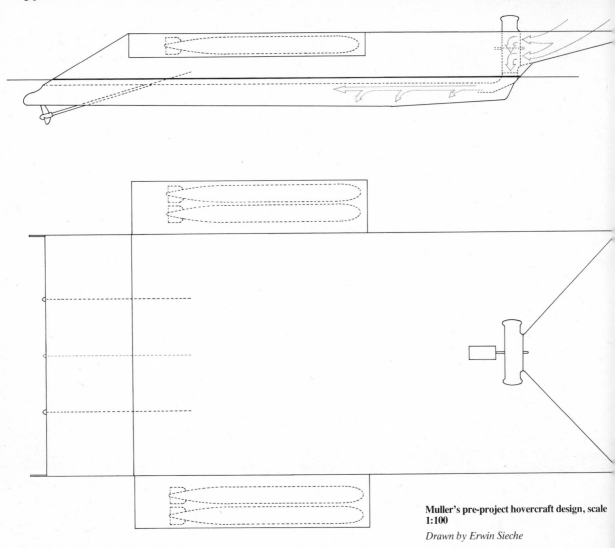

Muller's pre-project hovercraft design, scale 1:100

Drawn by Erwin Sieche

stem and stern. For the machinery Müller faced a problem as the only suitable engines with the required high power/weight ratio were aircraft engines. Since 1909 the *Österreichische Daimler-Motoren Gesellschaft* at Wiener Neustadt had produced the Austrodaimler engines, designed by Ferdinand Porsche – later to become famous as the constructor of the Volkswagen. These very reliable engines had now been developed to a point were they had reached 300hp and Müller, therefore, proposed to borrow obsolete 120hp engines from the Pola Naval Air Station (*Seeflugstation Pola*).

THE MTK APPRAISAL

The MTK judged Müllers tests as follows: '. . . the injection of air under the hull has a very positive influence on the resistance and, therefore, on the necessary amount of (propulsive) power which rises (initially) to maximum but decreases at higher speeds . . . The measured towing forces show that the resistance of the (proposed) hull form is so great that this vessel could only make 12kts . . . Stability is insufficient to enable operations even in light sea states . . . Tests should be carried out to ascertain if it would be better to situate the propellers deeper under the bottom or free from the stern.'

The MTK ordered the construction of an experimental hovercraft, now called the *Versuchsgleitboot*, to modified design, with dimensions of 13.0 x 4.0 x 0.36m (42.64 x 13.12 x 1.18ft), and a displacement of 7.8 tonnes (7.6 tons) and propelled by four 120hp 6-cyl Austrodaimlers to drive the propellers and one 65hp Austrodaimler for hovering. Comparison with the pre-project design shows some important differences:
1 A more streamlined hull profile.
2 Only the after section of the hull was to be lifted by the air cushion; the forward section would simply glide on the water surface.

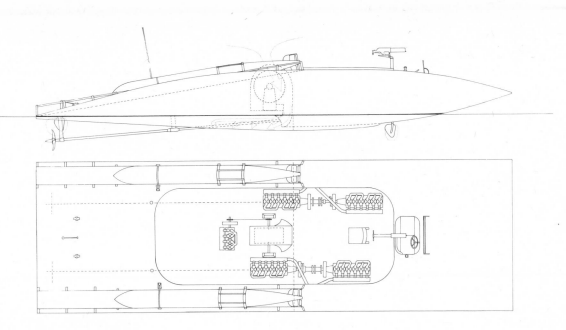

**Final MTK version of the experimental
Versuchsgleitboot, scale 1:100**

Drawing by Erwin Sieche

Torpedo launching trials.

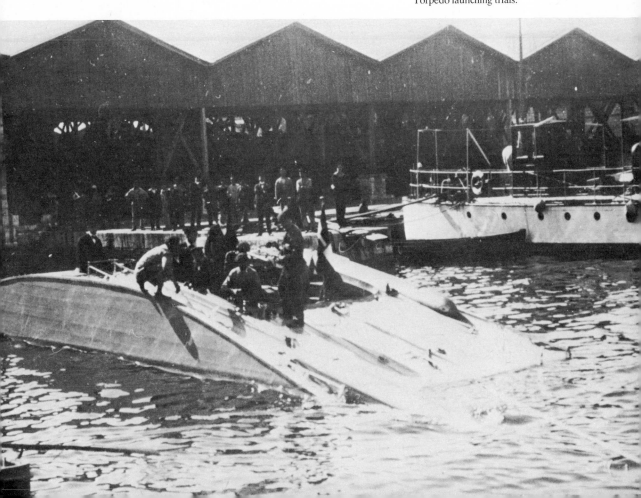

3 A more powerful surface propulsion plant.

4 Torpedoes situated inboard, placed in open chutes for sternward ejection.

The following describes the details of the design.

HULL

The MTK design had a rectangular hull of spindle-shaped profile, with the bottom divided, by a vertical step, into gliding and hover sections. To ensure eddyless air-injection a swallowtail-shaped duct was situated at this vertical step. The hull was built completely of wood but the torpedo chutes were lined with sheet metal. A forward rudder was positioned under the driver's cockpit and an after rudder near the stern, both on the centreline. As all standard formulas for the calculation of rudders and propellers (eg Hope's Formula, first published in *Engineering* in 1915) were not applicable, various rudder shapes and propellers from different suppliers (each differing in radius and inclination) were tested.

MACHINERY

Each pair of 120hp surface propulsion engines drove through a common gearbox to a single propeller shaft. They were placed in tandem and all exhaust gases were injected into the hover section, under the hull, to assist the 65hp hover engine.

ARMAMENT

A single 8mm Schwarzlose machine gun Mk (19)07/12 was mounted on the hull forward. The torpedo armament consisted originally of two 45cm weapons, each in an open chute arranged for launching over the stern by means of compressed air. Later a depth-charge thrower, for three small 6kg (13.23lb) bombs, was placed on the stern slope. Unfortunately, I have been able to locate neither plans nor photographs of this device.

CONSTRUCTION

The *Versuchsgleitboot* was built at Pola Navy Yard to the following schedule:

17.6.1915: Start of preparatory work

1.7.1915: Keel laid
16.9.1915: All fittings on board
2.9.1915: Launched
3.9.1915: First trials

THE TEST RESULTS

As might be expected, since this was an experimental vessel some minor problems were encountered but they are not discussed here as they do not directly concern the success or failure of the basic concept. These difficulties were with such items as the ignition, the gearbox and so on. Tests with the originally planned 45cm torpedoes showed poor results, so it was decided to switch to the more reliable 35cm torpedoes. (The technical and tactical problems of firing a torpedo from a high-speed vessel are discussed in the next section.)

More interesting are the results of the world's first hovering trials (see Table 1). When hovering, without forward movement, the area abaft the bottom step was completely filled with air, the hull rising out of the water by 15cm, giving an apparent displacement reduction from 6.3 to 3 tonnes. The air flowing out sternwards also produced a 3kt forward speed. The tests showed that the greatest improvement of speed lay between 16 and 24kts, the true speed increase being about 4–5kts. At higher speeds the improvement provided by hovering decreased to between 2.4 and 2.7kts. Owing to the hull form, the boat came out of the water at speeds above 20kts, even when hovering was not employed. As we will see later, the MTK had to decide if the additional speed of about 2kts was worth the extra weight involved in the provision of a fifth engine, a fan and the additional fuel. When judging the maximum speed, it must be kept in mind that the fastest potential opponents of the *Versuchsgleitboot* were the Italian *Motoscafi anti sommergibili* (MAS, or motor anti submarine boat), capable of only 24kts, or, in the case of a torpedo-carrying hovercraft attacking a convoy, Allied escorts capable of 28-30kts. However, in the case of the Italian MAS, it is clear that what was really needed was a fast, armoured, motor gun boat and not a hovercraft.

TACTICAL EMPLOYMENT

At first sight a small high-speed boat appears to be an ideal torpedo-carrying vessel, but on closer examination we find that the release of the torpedo becomes a problem when the speed of the launching vessel approaches that of the torpedo itself (the contemporary Austrian 45cm torpedo was capable of 38–40kts). In principle there are four different methods of launching torpedoes, regardless of the equipment used (torpedo tubes, launching frames, chutes and other devices):

1 Over the bow. Here the vessel has to slow down to let the torpedo run on ahead.

2 Over the stern. Here the vessel has to do a half-turn at the height of its attack, showing her full broadside to the target. Unless she slows down, this turn has, necessarily, to be of large tactical diameter. In addition, the Austrian tests showed that a fast-running boat leaves a wake of disturbed water which was liable to upset the accurate run of a standard torpedo.

3 Over the side, parallel to the hull. This could be achieved by dropping the weapon from clamps (as in the Italian MAS) or outboard containers (as in Müller's pre-project design). Using this method, attack was possible at both high and low speeds.

4 Launch in forward direction, from fixed or trainable inboard torpedo tubes. Not suitable for a small 40ft vessel.

THE FINAL JUDGEMENT

On the 20 October 1916 the board of the MTK met for a final judgement on Müller's idea, the boat and the results. For this naval constructor Dipl Ing Max Szombathy prepared a paper entitled *Schiffbauliche Bemerkungen* which is quoted below as it is much clearer and more professional than the final 'official' document.

'The basic idea proved practical and, from this point of view, the experimental vessel was successful. Military use of the boat is not recommended due to the following disadvantages:

1 The boat is not seaworthy. The

TABLE 1: LIST OF TRIAL RESULTS

Date	Displacement (tonnes)	Type	Propeller Diameter (mm)	Without air		With air		Speed increase (kts)
				Rpm	Speed (kts)	Rpm	Speed (kts)	
18.1.16	6.3	Zeise	630	780	20.4	–	–	–
29.11.15	6.5	Zeise	630	860	24.0	–	–	–
29.11.15	6.5	Zeise	630	1150	30.9	–	–	–
7.12.15	6.3	Zeise	630	1150	30.9	1200	32.6	2.7
7.12.15	7.5	Zeise	630	980	24.5	1200	29.7	5.2
7.1.16	6.5	Bauer	580	900	20.9	1000	30.0	3.1
16.1.16	6.5	MTK	820	690	22.8	–	–	–
21.1.16	6.4	MTK	820	710	22.8	960	26.9	4.1
23.1.16	6.4	MTK	820	915	25.9	1020	28.8	2.9
25.1.16	6.4	MTK	750	950	27.2	1035	29.6	2.4
28.1.16	6.4	MTK	750	1000	26.1	1175	27.7	1.6
29.1.16	6.3	MTK	750	1040	27.3	1150	30.5	3.2
31.1.16	6.3	MTK	690	1070	27.7	–	–	–
1.2.16	6.3	MTK	690	1100	28.8	1190	32.4	3.6
2.2.16	6.3	MTK	690	1060	29.2	1170	30.9	1.7
4.2.16	6.4	MTK	690	980	27.9	1060	30.1	2.2
6.2.16	6.4	MTK	660	1000	27.9	1100	31.15	3.25
7.2.16	6.3	MTK	660	1050	29.0	1120	30.4	1.4
9.2.16	6.4	MTK	660	1100	28.85	1200	31.0	2.15
10.2.16	6.4	MTK	660	1210	29.9	1310	32.3	2.4
13.2.16	6.4	MTK	690	1300	31.9	–	–	–

Note: at every new trial the pitch of the propeller blades was changed to obtain as much data as possible. The Zeise propellers came from Zeise at Hamburg/Altona; the Bauer-Wagner propellers from Ing C Bauer/Berlin; and the MTK propellers were a genuine development of the *Marinetechnisches Komitee.*

The 'Versuchsgleitboot' shortly before torpedo lauching trials with the original 45cm torpedoes.

broad, snub bow would require speed reduction in heavy seas and might lead to hull stress.

2 The boat is open, so rain and sea spray might disturb both electric ignition and the carburettors.

3 The boat has no bulkheads and a single leak could cause the total loss of the vessel.

4 The engines are not silenced which could lead to premature detection in night attacks.

5 The engines have no self-starters and it is a rather involved process to start them by crank. However, if the engines are kept in neutral when the vessel is stopped, to avoid the need for re-starting, they become over-oiled.

6 Torpedo launching over the stern is unsatisfactory, as the boats turning radius at high speed is too great.

8 The torpedo suffers from wide deviations when ejected at high speed due to propeller turbulence. It cannot stabilise itself and jumps out of the water or dives to great depth.

8 The throwing of depth-charges is

satisfactory but the minimum burst distances should be checked.'

SYNOPSIS

'The vessel has been built to run basic trials. For military use a number of modifications would be necessary. This would mean a complete rebuilding which would not however alter the boat's bad seaworthiness. In addition the crew should undergo special training. At present and in the existing form the boat cannot be recommended for military use.'

Based on this document, and the subsequent discussion thereof, the board judged that:

1 The boat was insufficient in terms of shipbuilding technology, was not seaworthy, and was difficult to handle.

2 The boat was unarmoured, open and without bulkeads.

3 The noise of the unsilenced engines would warn an enemy of its approach.

4 The speed, in full load condition, was too slow (!)

5 The torpedo ejection over the

stern was inefficient and the turning circle at high speed was so great that it would cost vital time in operational use.

6 The boat accelerated and stopped badly.

7 The boat could not carry out exact depth-charging, as visibility over the stern was not good enough at high speed.

8 The action radius was too small (120nm).

9 The boat was no substitute for a seaworthy, armoured, motorboat. '. . . But vessels of this or a similar type may be of value for the Navy if they can achieve a reliable speed of 40kts, at a sufficient action radius, and can carry a 1200kg (2645.54lb) warload . . .'

Some of the comments of the board are rather surprising or, at least, in contradiction with earlier comments. For example, earlier reports spoke of good handling capabilities and commented that it was not necessary to install reversing gear as the manoeuverability was sufficient. Considering the details of enemy

high-speed craft, the argument about insufficient speed seems not to have been throughly discussed. Nevertheless, the basic intrinsic value of the hovercraft has not changed during the last 53 years. A modern hovercraft is, like its remote predecessor, a vulnerable weapon carrier, suitable only for special missions, and needs very special maintenance and care.

The story of the *Versuchsgleitboot* ends prosaically: the engines were sent back to the Aviation Arsenal in Vienna and the hull was probably cannibalised during the following years. The last remnants of the world's first hovercraft may well have ended as firewood in the stoves of Pola.

DAGOBERT MÜLLER VON THOMAMUEHL

Müller was born on 24 July 1880 at Trieste. His father was the 'KuK chief engine constructing engineer' (*KuK oberstar Maschinenbauingenieur*) at Pola and he soon became interested in a naval career and, as we will see, was

later to have some brilliant engineering ideas.

In 1895 he entered the Pola Naval College (*Marineakademie*) and in 1899 was promoted to cadet. On the outbreak of the First World War he was commander of torpedo-boat *60T* but later became commander of torpedo-boat *93F*. It was during this time that he developed his ideas for the world's first hovercraft. Subsequently, he became the first commander of the newly formed Navy Diver's School, where he invented a new diving apparatus and became the first man to reach a depth of 64m (210ft) without using an armoured suit.

At the end of the war he founded the Torpedo Department of the Austrian Navy and became its first commander, initiating a series of trials in the launching of torpedoes from aircraft. He also developed, together with the Viennese physician Dr Dipl Ing Thirring, a system to secure harbour entrances against penetration by enemy forces by using a barrier composed of light beams. The system was first

produced by Carl Zeiss at Jena but later Siemens-Halske bought the licence. Today the use of photo-electric cells for early warning of or for measuring, whatever passes has become commonplace, but few would think that this idea was first developed as a harbour security device.

His postwar fate mirrors the fate of an inhabitant of a former multinational empire. As his family was of Sudentenland origin, he became a Czechoslovakian subject, but he settled in Yugoslavia as he had married and built up a trading company there. In 1934 he thus became a German subject, when Hitler brought the Sudentenland into the Reich. After the Second World War he settled at Klagenfurt, in Austria, where he died on 10 January 1956. According to his testament he was buried at Pola.

Trials at 17kts – note the air escaping at the sides and under the bows of the vessel.

The Twin 12 inch BVI Mounting

drawn by Peter Hodges

The accompanying drawing shows in section a typical twin 12in barbette mounting of the pre-dreadnought period, and is one of a large number of illustrations which appear in *The Big Gun* by Peter Hodges, due for publication by *Conway Maritime Press* in February 1981. The 12in BVI was fitted in the British battleships *Formidable, Implacable, London, Bulwark, Duncan, Montague, Russell, Cornwallis* and *Queen*. Its principle advantage over earlier mountings was the provision of a new gun, the 12in MkIX, which was a 50 ton, 40 calibre weapon with a muzzle velocity of 2650fps giving a maximum effective range of 15,000yds. For comparison the previous MkVIII gun was of 46 tons and $35\frac{1}{2}$ calibres long, and had a muzzle velocity of 2525fps giving a maximum effective range of 13,800yds. Both weapons had a maximum elevation of $13\frac{1}{2}°$ and employed the standard 850lbs shell but with the MkIX the charge weight was increased from 200 to 254lbs of cordite

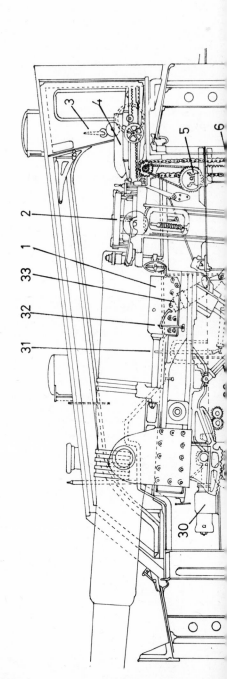

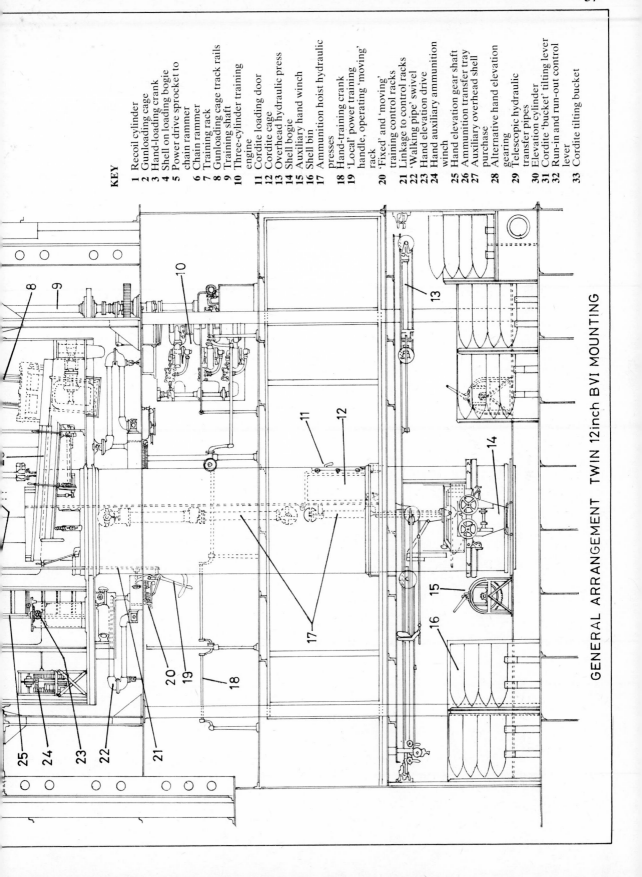

KEY

1 Recoil cylinder
2 Gunloading cage
3 Hand-loading crank
4 Shell on loading bogie
5 Power drive sprocket to chain rammer
6 Chain rammer
7 Training rack
8 Gunloading cage track rails
9 Training shaft
10 Three-cylinder training engine
11 Cordite loading door
12 Cordite cage
13 Overhead hydraulic press
14 Shell bogie
15 Auxiliary hand winch
16 Shell bin
17 Ammunition hoist hydraulic presses
18 Hand-training crank
19 'Local' power training handle, operating 'moving' rack
20 'Fixed' and 'moving' training control racks
21 Linkage to control racks
22 'Walking pipe' swivel
23 Hand elevation drive
24 Hand auxiliary ammunition winch
25 Hand elevation gear shaft
26 Ammunition transfer tray
27 Auxiliary overhead shell purchase
28 Alternative hand elevation gearing
29 Telescopic hydraulic transfer pipes
30 Elevation cylinder
31 Cordite 'bucket' tilting lever
32 Run-in and run-out control lever
33 Cordite tilting bucket

GENERAL ARRANGEMENT TWIN 12inch BVI MOUNTING

The British 'B' Class Submarine Part 1

by Michael Wilson

HMS/M *B2*. Note that the casing stops well short of the bow.
CPL

The 'B' class submarines represented the third generation of submarine design and production in the Royal Navy. The first of the class was included in the 1903–04 Programme and the last was completed in July 1906, yet these submarines, with their early design and equipment, were able to take part in active operations against the enemy during the First World War, the oldest RN submarines to be so engaged. Elsewhere it would have been comparable to asking the RFC or the RNAS to fly a Bleriot in 1916 to spot for the artillery!

The success of the original Holland-type submarines, built between February 1901 and January 1903, led the Admiralty to place further orders with Vickers, the shipbuilding company at Barrow. With the 1903–04 Programme it was originally planned to build ten submarines of the 'A' class *(A5–A14)*, but later the last boat of the batch was cancelled and the first of a new and improved class *(B1)* was substituted. *B1* was ordered on 24 March 1904 and, as the first of a new class, must have been given some priority in the building yard since she was launched before *A7* and later boats and completed on 16 April 1905, the same day as *A7*. A further ten boats of this class were ordered in the following year's programme, the last *(B11)* being completed in July 1906.

Whilst the 'A' class were an improvement on the prototype Hollands they were still limited in speed, endurance and seakeeping qualities, being liable to plunge from the surface in a swell. The 'B' class, improving on these shortcomings, were nearly 40ft longer, at over 140ft overall, while their beam was increased by 10in, giving a surface displacement of 287 tons, an increase of 100 tons.

DIVING PERFORMANCE

Figures for the time required by the early classes of submarine to dive are not available but it seems to have been far from a rapid process. Indeed, in 1916 Commander Tompkinson, when writing from Venice asking that the 'B' class

there be replaced by more modern boats, stated that they required about three minutes to dive from running on the surface on the petrol engine – too long in a war area where enemy patrols were active. Whilst the importance of diving as quickly as possible was recognised, not least by the submariners themselves, the actual process of diving in this class, as in the earlier ones, could be lengthy due to the shape of the boat and the Kingston valve fitted tanks, which meant that too rapid an intake of water tended to make the boat dive out of control. In addition, it was common practice to increase the surface buoyancy by pumping out some of the water from the trimming tanks and this, too, increased the diving time.

In the case of the Hollands and the 'A' class, only one set of hydroplanes, or diving rudders as they were then known, had been fitted, and these were aft. Depth-keeping, or diving and surfacing, was effected by angling the boat and driving it to the required depth. The next stage was for another set of hydroplanes to be fitted on the forward sides of the conning tower and this was done while building in *B1, B2* and *B3* although not in *B4* (records do not show whether or not this occurred with *B5–B11)*. Bow hydroplanes came in later still and were eventually fitted retrospectively to the class. Indeed, it was not until January 1916 that the last boat, *B6*, was so fitted, the equipment then having to be sent out from England, and the work was done by the Italians at Venice.

During the first decade of this century, when the 'B' class was built, the methods of computing hull strength were much less of an exact science than they are now, and consequently it is more difficult for the historian to quote a diving depth for these early submarine classes than it is for the more modern boats. During construction the hulls of the 'B' class, in common with the boats of the 'A' and 'C' classes, were tested to a pressure of 35psi by filling the hull with water and then applying external pressure. Despite

this nominal testing for a 100ft diving depth, the normal maximum operating depth was considered to be 50ft. Even so, the needs of war made exceptions and *B1* recorded reaching 95ft, while *B10* was deliberately taken to 60ft to pass through an Austrian minefield.

MACHINERY

The main engine fitted in the 'B' class was a 16-cylinder petrol engine manufactured by Vickers and developed from a similar engine designed by Wolseley and fitted in the earlier classes. In practice this gave a maximum speed of 12kts and an endurance of 740 miles. The dangers of using a petrol engine in a boat with restricted ventilation were only too well known, and great care had to be taken at all times to prevent an accident. The ease with which this could happen was demonstrated on board *A5*, which blew up at Queenstown in February 1905 when a spark from the motors ignited the petrol-laden atmosphere. Obviously the adoption of diesel-powered engines would have been much safer, but when the 'B' class were ordered the reliability and performance of these engines was unproven, the first only going to sea in *A13* which was completed after the last of the 'B' class.

The main motor was fitted on the same single shaft as the engine and so could be used for starting the engine as well as for dived propulsion. It had a triple armature, compound wound, and the working voltage was only 100. The battery consisted of 159 chloride cells with a designed discharge rate of 3hrs 45min at full speed. However, during the life of these boats the capacity of the battery was constantly being increased as the design of batteries was improved. Indeed, it was due mainly to the fact that *B11* had recently been fitted with a new battery of greater endurance that she, rather than any of the other British and French boats that were present, was selected for the first attempt at forcing the Dardenelles in late 1914.

B1 with a canvas screen rigged to her small conning-tower platform.

CPL

1

2

1 HMS/M *B1* as built.

CPL

2 The submarine depot at Gosport (HMS *Dolphin*) in the early years of the century. In the foreground is a line of 'A' class boats with a 'B' class in the extreme right. The next row consists entirely of 'B' class vessels while the boats beyond them are mostly, if not all, of the 'C' class. All eleven of the 'B' class are in this photograph.

3 A vessel of the first Royal Navy submarine class, *Holland No 2*, alongside the submarine depot ship (ex torpedo-gunboat) *Hazard*.

CPL

ARMAMENT
The submarines of this class were built with two 18in bow torpedo tubes, fitted side by side and angled slightly downwards. The bow caps were hand operated. As originally designed they were intended to carry two spare torpedoes but over the years, with improvements elsewhere involving extra weight, it became necessary not to embark the reload torpedoes or else an equivalent quantity of fuel could not be carried. No gun was fitted.

ACCOMMODATION

Living conditions, for the complement of two officers and 13 ratings, were undoubtedly bad, since despite the increase in size over the earlier Hollands and the 'A' class there was no corresponding improvement in amenities. It was accepted that the crew could live onboard for short periods only but this was thought to be acceptable since the role of these boats was purely defensive. Although ventilation was provided for the battery there was no living area ventilation and there could have been little free circulation of fresh air. Fumes from the engine permeated the boat, and mice were carried to detect any high concentration of carbon monoxide inside the boat from the engine exhaust. There were no dividing bulkheads and no specific accommodation spaces, the crew resting or sleeping where they could when at sea.

PARTICULARS OF 'B' CLASS SUBMARINES

Length (oa)	142ft 2½in
Beam	12ft 7in
Draught	11ft 2in
Displacement	287 tons (surface); 316 tons (submerged)
Machinery	One 16-cylinder Vickers petrol engine (600hp), one electric motor
Fuel	15½ tons
Speed	12kts (surface); 6.5kts (submerged)
Armament	2–18in TT (bow), 4 torpedoes
Complement	2 officers, 13 ratings

The *A11*, last boat of the preceding 'A' class; note the compass binnacle on the casing abaft the conning tower.

CPL

Part 2 of this article will cover the war operations of the class.

The Development of Radar in the Royal Navy 1945~60

by Alastair Mitchell

The island of the newly completed aircraft carrier *Eagle* on 18 March 1952. The triple-cheese aerial of one of her two Type 982 sets is mounted at the after end of the superstructure – it was later replaced by an aerial of different design. To the left of this aerial is one of the ship's CRBF directors, which utilised the close-range gunnery set Type 262, and forward of that the aerial of Type 983. On the extreme right can be seen one of the aerial nacelles of Type 275 on the roof of the after 4.5in gun director; on the mainmast is the frame aerial of Type 960, which was of the same design as that provided for Type 281; and on the foremast the cheese aerial of Type 293Q and on the foretopmast the standard YE homing beacon aerial.

CPL

During six years of war, shipborne radar had expanded from the first simple low-frequency air-warning set to a point where a modern battleship or cruiser carried up to three warning radars and as many as 10 to 15 gunnery sets, as well as IFF and radar search and countermeasures systems. Unfortunately, due to the rapid rate of development, much of the equipment fitted was already obsolescent, while the advent of jet-propelled aircraft and guided weapons called for new designs giving longer ranges, greater accuracy and the ability to track targets through 'clutter' and enemy jamming.

Work on new systems and techniques was proceeding rapidly in Britain and the United States in 1945 but the surrender of Japan in September of that year removed much of the impetus and, in the postwar run-down of the defence establishment, a re-appraisal of future needs was carried out. In Britain, the bleak economic outlook forced a policy of making do with

what was fitted while carrying on with a limited programme of research and development.

LONG-RANGE AIR SURVEILLANCE

In 1945 the fleet relied mainly on the metric Type 281 series, backed up by the earlier Type 79/279 for air warning. In its final form the Type 281 gave reasonable cover out to about 100 miles against aircraft at medium heights, whilst the 79 series provided good cover at higher angles. Battleships and cruisers carried either one or the other but all fleet carriers and the new *Colossus* class light fleet carriers were fitted with both in an attempt to obtain gap-free cover.

To cope with low-flying aircraft and to provide accurate tracking facilities, most ships were fitted with the 70cm Type 277 and its associated target indicating set, Type 293. The 277 had a range of approximately 30 miles and could also be used as a height-finder at short range, although its value in this latter role was severely limited by its relatively wide 4.5° vertical beam. One or two ships, including the carriers *Indomitable* and *Ocean*, were fitted with the American fighter-direction (FD) set SM-1 which had a better performance and was a much more accurate height-finder. However, it was a very heavy and complex radar which was being replaced in the US Navy by the lighter and simpler Type SP so, with the end of the war, plans for further installations were dropped. The *Indomitable* had her SM-1 removed during her 1948–50 refit but *Ocean* retained hers into the 1950s

In a 1945 review of the ability of the radars then in service to meet projected operational requirements, it was considered that Types 79 and 281 would have to be replaced. The Type 79B, with its poor low-angle performance, was obsolete. In addition, its wide beam and manual aerial rotation ruled out the use of PPI displays which were essential in modern warfare. The Type 281BQ had been modified for PPIs but the display was poor, due to the 35° beamwidth, and it was easily jammed. Furthermore, after five years of continuous modification, there were problems with its reliability.

TYPE 960

The Type 79/281 replacement under development at the end of the war was Type 960. Based on the 281 design, it operated in the same frequency band and was essentially a cleaned-up version of the earlier set. Various improvements gave a range of 130 – 150 miles and the use of a shorter pulse length improved the PPI and Skiatron display pictures. (The Skiatron was a horizontal projection PPI display used for air direction.) On most ships it was intended that the existing 281BQ aerial be used, but for fleet carriers a large mattress array was envisaged producing a beam width of 17° and a range of 200 miles. In the event, this aerial never materialised, and the Type 960 used the 281BQ aerial throughout its operational life in the RN.

The reconstructed carrier *Victorious*, seen here on trials in 1958, was the first ship to be fitted with the 3D radar Type 984. The aerial array, with its large drum shaped mounting, is fitted above the bridge. She also carried Tacan (at the masthead), Type 293Q, Type 974 and a carrier approach radar.

MoD, courtesy AD Baker III

With so little money available, plans for replacing the obsolete Type 79Bs and 281s with Type 960 were abandoned after the war. Between 1945 and 1950 few radar updates were carried out, and cruisers coming out of refit in 1948 still carried Type 79B. Even as late as 1950, the cruiser *Ceylon* commissioned for service in the East Indies with an old two-aerial Type 281 system. The carriers in commission also kept their 79B/281BQ systems until about 1954 and both types only passed out of service as the unmodernised wartime ships went into reserve around the mid-1950s.

As far as is known the first major ship to be fitted with Type 960 was the battleship *Vanguard*, completed in May 1946, and thereafter the set slowly trickled into service as the few ships selected for modernisation entered service or new construction joined the fleet. Among the former were the cruisers *Newcastle* and *Birmingham*, whilst new ships so fitted included the *Eagle* and *Albion* class carriers, the *Tiger* class cruisers and the new AA and AD frigates.

The Type 960 provided long-range warning for the fleet throughout the 1950s and into the early 1960s, when it was gradually replaced by the 200MHz Type 965. For over 20 years the old four-dipole array had served the navy well, and its passing marked the end of the age of relatively simple, straightforward radars.

TYPES 277/293
Although little in the way of new equipment was being fitted in the immediate postwar period, development work continued at the Admiralty Signal Establishment (ASE) on the design of new systems and on improvements to existing equipments. One of the main needs was for better FD sets than the existing Types 277/293. The main requirements were longer range and a better height-finding capability. The metric Type 960 was considered adequate for long-range warning but, to achieve the high accuracies required for modern interception techniques, centimetre radar was essential. As there were increasing limitations on simply boosting transmitter power (to double the range the power had to be increased 16-fold) the main effort went into producing better aerials and improving receiver designs.

Several lines of development were pursued but the first to appear was the 'Q' version of the existing Types 277/293. In the case of the Type 277Q, a new aerial array, Type ANU, was designed to reduce the vertical beamwidth. The size of the aerial was increased, resulting in an 8ft spherical paraboloid with clipped sides. As a result the vertical beamwidth was reduced from the 4.5° of the 'P' version to 2.5° making the 'Q' a much more useful height-finder.

A new aerial was also designed for the Type 293 target indicator set. The basic cheese array was retained but the sweep diameter was increased, thereby reducing the beamwidth from 2.6° to 2.0°, to obtain better bearing accuracy and resolution. In both cases the actual radar equipment was unchanged and the differences in performance were due solely to the new aerial systems. The two types were intended to be complementary, the Type 293Q being used to put the 277Q height-finder on to the target. The range remained in the region of 30 – 35 miles, the main improvement being in the increased accuracy obtained, especially in height-finding.

The 'Q' version of the 277/293 went into production in the late 1940s and the fleet carrier *Indomitable*, given a partial modernisation in 1948–50, was one of the first major ships equipped with the new set. She joined the Home Fleet in mid-1950 with a radar outfit consisting of two 277Qs, mounted fore and aft on the island for all-round cover, a 293Q on the foremast and a 281 or 960 on the mainmast. The layout of the sets became standard in all carriers and remained so until the introduction of the large Type 965 array forced a change.

The rest of the active carrier force, including *Illustrious* and the light fleets, were also fitted with Type 277Q by the early 1950s, but not all received the full package. Of the *Colossus* class only *Warrior* was given an interim modernisation, in 1952–53 , coming out of Devonport with two Type 277Qs mounted on a new lattice mast. However, the *Majestic* class carriers, completing for the Commonwealth navies, were given the full Type 277Q/293Q systems.

By the time the 'Q' versions were coming into service all the wartime battleships were in reserve and the only ship in service, *Vanguard*, was not updated. However, a limited cruiser modification programme was undertaken, starting with *Newcastle* and *Birmingham* in 1950. The programme carried through until 1957, ending with *Belfast*, and all the ships included in the programme were fitted with the now standard warning outfit of Types 277Q and 293Q on the foremast and Type 960 on the mainmast.

TYPES 982/983
Even as the Type 277 was being introduced into service in 1944, it was recognised that more powerful and accurate radars were required for fighter-direction and interception, and ASE began design work on new centimetric radars with a better performance than the Type/293 series. Two separate sets were again envisaged, Type 980 for horizontal surveillance and Type 981 for height-finding. Both operated in the 10cm band and, using fully stabilised aerials, it was hoped that a range of 60 miles could be achieved, together with a height-finding capability at maximum range.

Despite the end of the war, development work continued and led ultimately to the manufacture of the Type 982 and 983 radars, which entered service in the new fleet carrier *Eagle* in 1951. Type 982 was the fighter-direction set and, initially, was equipped with a large stabilised treble-cheese aerial. The actual radar equipment was much the same as in the Type 277Q, but the more sophisticated aerial array theoretically gave much better cover and, being stabilised, greater

1 The island structure of *Indomitable,* after her 1948-50 reconstruction, with a Hawker Sea Fury in the foreground. On the extreme left is the back of one of her directors with the aerials of Type 285P on its roof – above the compass platform is the 'clipped edge' dish aerial of Type 277Q and, on the short pole mast to port and forward of the funnel, the aerial of the YE homing beacon.

Fleet Air Arm Museum, Yeovilton

2 A close up of the forward superstructure of the frigate *Berwick* at Portsmouth in the early 1960s. Note the main director with its twin Type 275 radar aerial nacelles, one for receiving and one for transmitting. Abaft the director, on its short lattice tower, is the aerial for Type 277Q, and on the foremast platform of the frigate beyond *Berwick* is the cheese aerial of Type 293Q.

J A Roberts

accuracy. The beamwidth was 2°
(approx) and the range was
probably in the region of 60 miles, if
the design requirements were met.
Type 983 was intended as a
height-finder and employed a large
vertical parabolic array, also
stabilised, that gave a vertical
beam-width of 1.5.° The
stabilisation of the aerials ensured
greater accuracy but led to a
considerable increase in weight,
which restricted the fitting of the
sets to carriers and specialised ships.

Although both the carriers
Centaur and *Ark Royal* ran trials
with the treble-cheese Type 982
fitted, the system had obviously not
proved a success in *Eagle* and in

1955 a new aerial was fitted. Less
ambitious, the new aerial was not
stabilised. It was almost an
elongated Type 293, consisting of a
26.5ft long narrow parabolic
trough, giving a beamwidth of only
1°, fed from a slotted waveguide.
Both *Eagle* and *Ark Royal* were
fitted with two of each system,
whilst the smaller *Albion* class
carried two Type 982s but only one
Type 983 height-finder. In addition,
all the new carriers had Type 293Q
on the foremast for directing the
ship's armament and Type 960 for
long-range warning. Type 982 was
subsequently fitted in the new AD
frigates of the *Salisbury* class where,
on the smaller displacement, it was

The newly completed battleship *Vanguard*
out of Portsmouth harbour on 4 December
1946. She was the first ship to be fitted with
radar Type 960, but the aerial had not been
fitted at the time this photograph was taken
(the frame aerial was latter added at the
maintopmast head). The other sets carried
included Type 277Q (aerial on foremast
starfish), 293Q (aerial on foretopmast head),
268 for navigation (aerial – not visible in this
photograph – on mainmast), 274 (aerials on
roofs of fore and aft DCTs), 275 (aerials on
secondary DCTs) and 262 (aerials on
close-range AA mountings). The platform on
'B' turret was added for the 1947 Royal Tour
to South Africa and temporarily replaced the
twin 40mm STAAG mounting normally
carried in that position.

CPL

teamed with the lighter Type 277Q height-finder. Both systems served well into the 1970s with the diminishing carrier force and, indeed, the AS carrier *Bulwark* has carried the Type 982 into the 1980s.

TYPE 984

The advantages of having a radar on board ship that could scan both horizontally and vertically were obvious. If it could be made to give the same degree of accuracy as the conventional types and achieve a reasonable range, then a great deal of space and weight could be saved. Although the disadvantages of having all your eggs in one basket were recognised, work started in 1948 on the design of the 3-D Type 984 radar. With the technology available in the late 1940s the result rather defeated the object of the

exercise. The aerial system for the Type 984 was certainly impressive, consisting of a large 'searchlight' array approx 15ft in diameter. This enormous rotating structure housed a series of electronic lenses that produced two beams, one relatively wide that scanned at low angles, the other a pencil beam that scanned vertically as the structure rotated. The sheer size of the system precluded its widespread use and, indeed, only three carriers were ever fitted with it.

The Type 984 was introduced into service in the reconstructed carrier *Victorious* in 1958. Apart from the target indicating Type 293Q and the gunnery control radar, the only additional radar equipment fitted was a small navigational set. New displays were fitted to improve tracking and fighter-direction capabilities. As no long-range metric radar was fitted,

ranges in excess of 100 miles were obviously anticipated, or else great reliance was to be place on AEW aircraft and cruiser escorts. The carrier *Hermes*, completed in 1959, was similarly equipped, but *Eagle* received a more comprehensive outfit, including a long-range Type 965, during her modernisation of 1960–64.

With only three sets ever fitted, and no further effort on the part of the RN to develop a 3-D system, it is probably true to say that the Type 984 was not a resounding success. With the technology available at the time, the set was too bulky and the enormous size and weight of the complex aerial severely limited the number of ships that could carry it, making it expensive to manufacture and maintain. The decision in 1966 to phase out the carrier force finally removed the necessity for such a radar in the fleet.

The guided-weapons trials ship *Girdle Ness* which provided the test bed for the 'Seaslug' missile system. From forward the aerials are a radar dish for missile guidance, of unknown designation, and Type 901 'beam riding' radar above the bridge; Type 293Q and VHF/DF on the foremast; Type 960 on the mainmast; and Types 983 and 982 aft.

MoD(N)

The *Ark Royal* in 1955 shows a similar radar outfit to that of *Eagle* except that Type 982 trough aerials have replaced the triple-cheese aerials at the fore and aft ends of the island, and the Type 293Q aerial has a higher, and clearer, position at the head of a lattice foremast.

MoD(N), courtesy Roger Chesneau

The light fleet carrier *Ocean* in August 1948, with the aerials of her US Type SM1 above the compass platform, Type 281 and 293 on the foremast platform and Type 279B on the mainmast.

Wright and Logan

COMBINED SURFACE/AIR WARNING RADAR

At the end of the war, ships were fitted with a variety of radars depending on their refit state and their intended area of operations. Ships proceeding to join the Pacific Fleet were normally given the latest Type 277/293, with destroyers carrying a Type 291PQ for air warning in lieu of the Type 79/281 fitted in bigger ships. The Type 291 had been introduced in 1942 and there were a number of variants, the final 'PQ' version having power-rotated aerials and PPI displays. As a surface warning set the 200MHz Type 291 suffered from the usual defects of short range and excessive beamwidth, inherent in low-frequency radars, and was rapidly being replaced by the 3cm Type 268. However, it was still considered to be of some value as an air warning set, and as a result it continued to be fitted on most small ships until 1951–52, despite the fact that its 35° beam gave a poor PPI picture which was useless for tracking aircraft. In 1952, with maintenance and spares becoming difficult and its usefulness decreasing, it was withdrawn from service without replacement. By 1951 the early centimetric Type 271–3 series had also passed out of service. With their manually rotated aerials, they were obsolete by 1945 and rapidly disappeared from the active fleet, although a few examples could still be seen on destroyers employed on secondary duties until 1949.

In 1950, the Type 277/293 reigned supreme in the fleet. The 'P' series was the most common version and was fitted on virtually every active ship of frigate size and above. On destroyers and frigates Type 293 was fitted when target-indication was required for the gunnery set, the type also providing air and surface warning on the majority. For AS work, the wider beam Type 277 was preferred and this was carried on the few *Loch* and *Castle* class frigates in commission.

With Type 293 fitted, the average destroyer could detect surface targets at 15 miles or so, and land masses at 20–30 miles, a useful feature in peacetime navigation. With a beamwidth of 2.6° the PPI picture was reasonably sharp, but the pulse length was too long to allow accurate coastal navigation. Normally, up to four PPIs were fitted, three for general plotting and one associated with the target-indication system. All were fitted with range markers, several different ranges being available. A ships heading marker and a compass ring driven from the gyro allowed either true or relative bearings to be determined.

With the withdrawal of the air warning Type 281 in 1951, most escorts had to make do with the Type 293, but the set did not really have the range to work effectively.

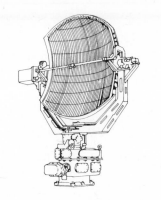

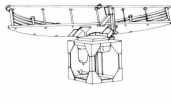

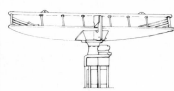

RADAR AERIALS: from top to bottom outfit ANU for Type 277Q, outfit AQR for Type 293P and outfit ANS for Type 293Q

Aircraft were of course detected, but the author recollects a number of occasions when very little warning of attacking aircraft was given and even one humiliating experience when a Sunderland flying boat lumbered up while the radar screens remained obstinately blank.

After trials in the destroyer *Scorpion*, the 293Q began to enter service in the smaller ships in 1951–52. First to be fitted were the fast frigate Type 15 conversions, with *Rocket* and *Relentless* in 1951, followed by the new *Daring* class destroyers. For the next decade it was the standard fit on all new and converted frigates.

With the emphasis on AS warfare throughout the 1950s, the new AS frigates and the Type 15 conversions were not fitted with an air warning set but were given both Types 277Q and 293Q. The 277Q was fitted in its original role as a surface warning set for detection of surfaced submarines or their 'snorkel' tubes, whilst the 293Q provided target information for the CRBF director controlling the 4in and 40mm armament.

NAVIGATION SETS
The aerial system for Type 293 was normally mounted at the masthead and required either a strong tripod or lattice tower to support it. On small ships, where space or topweight considerations made this impossible, the much smaller and lighter Type 268 was carried. Operating in the 3cm band, this set had been designed and built in Canada in 1944–45 and, after entering service in 1945, rapidly replaced the old metric Type 286

The FPB *Gay Bowman* in June 1955 with a Type 974 cheese aerial on her masthead.

Wright & Logan

systems on coastal craft, trawlers and the like. It was also fitted in several of the larger ships as a navigational aid and to the 'Hunt' class destroyers and *Algerine* class minesweepers in commission as they could not easily accommodate the larger Type 277/293 systems. With a 2° beamwidth and a range discrimination of 75yds, the Type 268 gave a sharp picture on its small PPI but the equipment was very complicated and badly designed for maintenance.

A much better set was required, and soon after the war development began of a new navigational radar for naval and merchant use. The set eventually adopted by the RN was the Decca Radar Type 974. Like the Type 268, the new set operated in the 3cm band and with the use of a 10in PPI could be described as the first of the high-definition marine radars. Operating on a frequency of 9345–9405 MHz, the transmitter had a power output of 7kW and a pulse length of 0.1 or 0.2 microseconds, at 1000 pulses per second. The aerial was a small double-cheese with separate transmitting and receiving sections. Fixed immediately below the aerial, and rotating with it, was a watertight box containing the transmitter output and receiver input sections. The combined layout saved a lot of waveguide plumbing and the need for a transmit/receive (T/R) switch, thereby avoiding the signal losses associated with both these items.

Maximum range was 25 miles and the minimum range was 25yds. With an aerial beamwidth of 2° and a range discrimination of 25yds, the radar picture was very clear and for the first time navigation and station-keeping purely by radar became possible. Starting in 1951, virtually every ship in the active fleet, from fleet carriers to inshore minesweepers, was fitted with Type 974. In the larger ships it was normally mounted on a small platform below the Type 293 or on top of the bridge. In smaller craft, where it was the only set fitted, it was usually mounted on a small lattice tower. The aerial position often produced a blind arc astern

but, as the set was mainly used for navigation, this presented few problems.

Like all centimetric sets it was badly affected by heavy rain which tended to blot out large areas of display, making target sighting and tracking difficult. The main failing of the set, nevertheless, was in the positioning of part of the radar equipment up the mast with the aerial. Failure of a component involved a climb up the mast and opening of the watertight box, often in foul weather, which inevitably prolonged the out-of-service time. However, a combination of funnel gases and the grim features of the captain on the bridge below often acted as a spur to the unfortunate radar mechanic. In 1954 a small slave display was supplied for fitting on the bridge, giving the officer of the watch a direct PPI picture. The Type 974 remained the main navigational radar in the fleet throughout the decade and well into the 1960s until gradually replaced by the Type 978.

GUNNERY RADAR

At the end of the war, most ships were equipped with various marks of the Type 282–285 series of 600MHz gunnery radars. Design work had begun in 1942 on centimetric replacements but by the end of the war only the low-angle Type 274, used for controlling the main armament of battleships and cruisers, had been fitted in any quantity. Operating in the 10cm band, Type 274 met practically all the staff requirements in regard to range, bearing accuracy and resolution, and no further development was envisaged in the postwar period. With the elimination of all the potential enemy surface fleets and the eclipse of the big gun by carrier aircraft, there was little point in developing the art any further. Thus Type 274 became the last low-angle gunnery radar developed for the RN and remained in service until the last of the wartime cruisers, *Belfast*, went into reserve in 1963.

Although Type 274 was not developed further, steps were taken to improve spotting accuracy by

developing a small 1.5cm set, the Type 931. In operation its beam was switched rapidly in a small arc across the target and, with its high resolution, produced very accurate measurements of range and bearing. Errors in both measurements could be read directly off the display and corrections made. Although prototypes were made, there is no information at present as to whether any sets were actually fitted for operational use.

The second 10cm set developed during the war was Type 275. Intended as a replacement for Type 285, it took longer to develop than the Type 274 due to the additional elevation information required. Further complications were involved in that it was combined with a new type of director that suffered production delays. The set eventually got to sea in 1945, initially in the new 'Battle' class destroyers and the battleship *Anson*, in time for the closing stages of the Pacific war, although its capabilities were unlikely to have been tested under actual combat conditions.

The Type 275 transmitted on a frequency of 3100MHz and, with a power output of 500kW, had an effective range of 30,000yds and an accuracy of 25yds. Intended for dual-purpose control, the aerial system was enclosed in two nacelles mounted either side of a Mk VI director, which could be trained in elevation. In the later 'Battles' and *Vanguard* the nacelles were mounted on top of the US Mk 37 director. Inside the nacelles were 4ft diameter parabolic dishes, one for transmitting and the other for receiving. The receiver aerial used an offset feed to produce a conical scan, which was equivalent to beam-switching in both planes. With and aerial beamwidth of 5° this gave an accuracy of 10 minutes of arc horizontally and vertically. 'A' scan displays were used for ranging with side-by-side displays for bearing and elevation. The actual radar equipment was split between the director and the room housing the display panels and associated equipment, all

interconnecting cables going up the director trunk.

The Type 275 performed well in service and continued to be fitted on modernised cruisers, destroyers and the new construction fleet carriers and frigates until the late 1950s, when it was replaced by the MRS-3 system. However, as with the warning radar, there were insufficient funds to equip all ships with Type 275, especially as a change of director was necessary. As a result, a considerable number of cruisers and destroyers, together with the *Black Swan* and 'Bay' class frigates, had to carry on with the old 285 system. The conversion of many of the 'O'–'Z' class destroyers to AS frigates, with the consequent removal of most of their guns and the associated director, solved the problem for some ships, but for the remaining old cruisers and frigates the problems of maintaining the obsolete equipment in the 1950s became insuperable. For some of the frigates, by then coming to the end of their useful lives, the Type 285 was allowed to expire, little or no effort being made to maintain it in a serviceable condition or to

provide the necessary spares back-up to do so. With the Type 285 on the way out, several of the 'Colony' class cruisers that had not undergone a full modernisation and were still active had it replaced by the American gunnery set AN/SPG34 as an interim measure. Developed at the end of the war, this 3cm set had a range of 20,000yds. The aerial was a rotating 30in diameter parabolic dish and in the 'Colony' class was mounted on the side of the 4in mountings. Several of the class, including *Kenya* and *Gambia*, carried this interim system until going into reserve in the late 1950s.

TYPE 262
Of the three centimetric systems developed in the latter part of the war, the one that excited most interest – even awe – was the Type 262. Designed as a replacement for the Type 282, it was intended to provide a blind-fire capability using a twin 40mm Bofors gun mounting, the whole system being known as a STAAG (Stabilised, Tachymetric Anti-Aircraft Gun) mounting. The unit was self-contained, with the

The cruiser Blake *at Barrow on 21 September 1961 shortly after completion. She carriers the newly introduced MRS3 fire control system, three of the directors of which can be seen, two above the bridge and one to starboard of the after funnel. Each carries the dish aerial of radar Type 903.*

Courtesy A Preston

guns, predictor and radar all on the one mounting. The radar operated in the 3cm band with a peak power output of 30kW. Conical scanning was used to obtain angular accuracy, the dish aerial being spun with its axis offset. Maximum target range was 7000yds, with auto-tracking at 5000yds. In normal operation the ship's Type 293 would indicate the incoming target's range and bearing, allowing the STAAG to be brought round to the approximate bearing. The Type262 radar then scanned 30° in azimuth in one second, the aerial being elevated 3° at the end of each sweep, at the same time exploring the area 750yds on each side of the indicated range 30 times a second. When the target was located the aerial automatically locked-on, the predictor ran into alignment with the mirror's axis of rotation, and the guns followed the predictor.

In theory, the system was perfect; in practice, it was a nightmare. The whole mounting was a mass of complicated electronic, electrical and mechanical parts, all subject to tremendous vibration when the guns fired. The radar units were mounted in waterproof containers on the gun mounting and, for each STAAG, 2 sets of Type 262 units were carried. Unfortunately several of the units were quite heavy, and changing a faulty unit on a mounting could be a protracted business. Breakdowns were frequent and much of the average ship's maintenance effort went into trying to keep the system serviceable.

Operationally, the system was seldom fully tested in peacetime. For safety reasons, complete blind-fire could not be tested under normal conditions, the old towing joke of 'I'm pulling the target, not pushing it' was only too true on some occasions, even in good visibility. Furthermore, controlled target drones were not normally available to the average ship, so aircraft shoots were usually carried out against towed sleeves using visual control and tracer ammunition. The Type 262 had a tendency to unlock and jump targets if a larger echo appeared close to the locked-on target; it would, therefore, have required a brave or foolhardy man to tow anything for a radar-controlled shoot.

Various modifications to improve the Type 262 were introduced after the war, but the main external change arrived in 1952 when the 'Q' version appeared on the new *Daring* class destroyers. In this version, the aerial was mounted immediately below the mounting's twin gun barrels in an attempt to reduce the effects of vibration. At the same time, the set began to be widely fitted in a separate, CRBF (Close Range Blind Fire) director. In this form it appeared on the newly converted Type 15 frigates and several of the new carriers.

In 1944 the Naval Staff asked for a new fire-control system, for guns up to 5.25in, to be developed as a follow-on to the US Mk 37, then being purchased for the later 'Battles' and the battleship *Vanguard*. It was agreed that conventional guns were only effective to about 7000yds and that

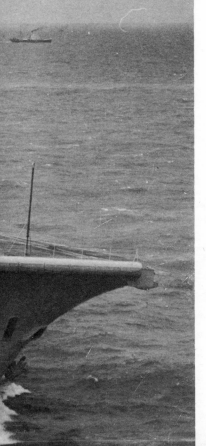

beyond that they only had a deterrent effect. With Type 262 catering for the medium range (effectively MRS-1 – Medium Range System 1 – in the new terminology), development work started on a long-range system, LRS-1. In parallel with this work, it had been recognised as early as 1943 that, against future high-speed aircraft, some form of guided weapon would be required for long-range defence, and by 1945 it had been decided that a missile system should be developed. A beam-riding weapon was agreed upon and a 3cm radar, Type 901, originally intended for the LRS-1 system, was adopted. The system, known initially as GMS-1, was begun and finally appeared as the Seaslug Mk I. The LRS-1 was abandoned in 1949 when it became

The carrier *Hermes* on completion of her full power trials on 18 November 1959. The circular aerial mounted on the lattice mast on the starboard side forward is for her VHF direction-finder. She also carries the aerials of Type 984, Type 293Q and Tacan.

CPL

The cruiser *Cumberland* in 1954 while serving as a training and trials ship. She carries the then experimental director of the MRS3 system, with its Type 903 radar dish, above the bridge.

CPL

obvious that missile systems would be essential for long-range defence. For close-range control of 4.5in guns a new control system, termed MRS-3, was developed, based on the US Mk 56 gun director designed at the end of the war. The Mk 56 used a 3cm radar, Mk 35, which had a range of 30,000yds and an accuracy of 10yds. The aerial system was a parabolic dish mounted on the director, which could train continuously in bearing and could elevate to 85°. By virtue of using a nutating waveguide feed (in simple terms, a nodding source of radio energy in front of the dish), target acquisition was by spiral scan and automatic tracking by conical scan. When developed for RN Service the radar was designated Type 903.

With so many new techniques involved and limited finance,

development times were long, with the result that little of this new equipment appeared in the fleet before 1960, although both Seaslug and MRS-3 were at sea in the late 1950s in the trials ships *Girdle Ness* and *Cumberland* respectively. However, one system that did enter service in the late 1950s was MRS-8. This, basically, was a development of the CRBF director with the predictor units replaced by a computer. Type 262 radar was employed, the 'R' modification version probably being used, and the system was intended to control both 4in and 40mm armaments. The system was fitted on the modernised cruiser *Belfast* and the AD destroyers of the 'Weapon' class.

The MRS-8 system, however, did not replace the Type 275 completely, and in the early 1960s 275 was fitted in several ships including the *Rothsay* class AS frigates and the modernised 'Ca' class destroyers, probably to give them a long-range surface gunnery capability. The MRS-3 system entered service in 1960 in the *Tiger* class cruisers and then in the 'Tribal' class frigates. Thereafter, Type 275 was not fitted, and it gradually disappeared from service as ships paid off or underwent modernisation, although a few examples still exist both in the RN and on ships transferred to foreign navies. Fitting of the Type 262 also ceased in about 1960 but, like the Type 275, the set soldiered on throughout the 1960s until the defence cuts at the end of that decade removed most of the older ships from the fleet.

IFF SYSTEMS

In 1945 virtually every ship in the fleet was equipped with IFF. Unlike the normal warning radars, which could be introduced into service piecemeal, an IFF system had to be brought into service on all ships and aircraft operating in a particular theatre of war in a very short space of time, if it was to work effectively. As a result the metric Mk III system, developed in the early part of the war, was still the only system in use. In the closing stages of the war, in addition to the normal 'A' band (171–182MHz) sets, a new 'G' band (209 MHz) set, with interrogators and transponders numbered Type 940 upwards, was being introduced in parallel with the old system. However, with the advent of peace, the new band was dropped and ships carried on with the old Type 242 and 253 interrogators and transponders. Fitting continued until the early 1950s but, with the limited number of codes that could be selected, the system was not secure and it gradually fell into disuse.

With the formation of NATO in 1950 a new system of IFF was agreed and a common specification for all equipments drawn up. The new frequency allocated was in the 1000MHz band and the system was known as Mk 10 IFF. The system operated by transmitting two pulses with a fixed time interval. When the transponder replied to the pulses, it sent a train of coded pulses into the space between the two re-transmitted pulses; in this way a total of 4096 different codes could be generated. The transponder had a omni-directional aerial and would reply to any ship or aircraft interrogating it in the correct mode. There were six different modes, identified by different spacings of the two interrogating pulses. Modes 1 and 2 were for IFF use, the remainder for combined civil/military use and civil use for air traffic secondary radar. In addition to normal IFF, there were facilities for ship-to-ship identification and a distress code.

The Mk 10 transponder transmitted on a frequency of 1030MHz with a power output of up to 5kW. The two pulses radiated were 0.8 microseconds long and spaced 5 microseconds apart in Mode 1 and 8 microseconds apart in Mode 2. The pulse repetition rate could vary between 200 and 450 pulses per second. Horizontal polarisation was adopted for the aerial systems and the RN fitted two types of narrow parabolic troughs. The larger of the two had a 9ft sweep diameter, giving a beamwidth of roughly 6°, and was normally mounted in line with the long-range radars Types 960 and, later, 965, and rotated in synchronism with them. On destroyers and frigates the aerial was roughly half the size, being approximately 4ft across, giving a beamwidth of 13–14°. It was normally mounted on a platform on the foremast below the navigational radar or on a small lattice mainmast. Common aerial working was used, and the same aerials received the replies from the transponder and passed them to the receiver and decoding units. Initially, manual decoding was used but later automatic decoding, employing a computer, was introduced. Fitting of the new IFF system began in 1956 in the RN, and the majority of active ships were equipped with it over the next few years.

Summing up, it is clear that the period 1945–60 was one of consolidation after the rapid advance of technology during the war. However, in that same period the transistor was born and the first step was taken along the path that was to lead to the present-day silicon-chip microprocessor, revolutionising radar systems on the way.

British Naval Guns 1880~1945 No1

By NJM Campbell

In previous issues of *Warship*, British rifled guns of 16in calibre and over have been described in detail. The following series will list those of under 16in, with briefer descriptions. In the first instance, breech loading (BL) guns not using a metal cartridge case and excluding those prior to 1880 are given. Weights of gun include those of the breech mechanism; muzzle velocities are 'new gun', with charge temperature 80°F, and ranges are for that muzzle velocity at the maximum elevation of the mounting concerned.

15in Mk I mounted in *Queen Elizabeth, Royal Sovereign, Renown* and *Courageous* classes, *Hood, Vanguard* and monitors of *Marshal, Terror* and *Roberts* classes; also in coast defence batteries at Singapore and Dover. Of standard wire-wound construction with tapered inner 'A' tube, 'A' tube, wire, 'B' tube with overlapping jacket, short breech ring, shrunk collar on 'A' tube and breech bush screwing into 'A' tube. Welin type breech block with hydraulically operated Vickers 'pure couple' mechanism. The original intention was to use the Elswick 3-motion short-arm mechanism, to reduce slamming, but gun E597, in which this was to be tried and which also had the 'B' tube and jacket combined in one, was delayed too long by a failed 'A' tube forging. The original mountings allowed 20° elevation but those in *Hood, Vanguard* and *Terror* and *Roberts* classes allowed 30°, while the mountings in *Queen Elizabeth, Warspite, Valiant, Renown* and *Marshal Soult* were later altered to 30°. The coast defence mountings allowed 50 or 55°. 186 guns were made.

Supercharges were available from 1942 for *Malaya* and the four surviving *Royal Sovereigns* to increase the range of their 20° mountings. They could also be fired by *Vanguard* but their only use appears to have been in the two coast defence guns at Dover. 1920lb shells had 3.05/4 calibre radius heads (crh) and the 1938lb shell 5/10crh.

15in Mk II Never made, but intended for one of the *King George V* class alternative designs with three 3-gun turrets. Construction would have been similar to that of the 14in Mk VII and 16in Mk II. The actual bore was to be 14.985in to reduce clearance and increase accuracy life with long 15in shells.

14in Mk I mounted in *Canada* (ex-Chilean *Almirante Latorre*), taken over in 1914–18 War. An Elswick design of standard wire-wound construction with 3-motion short-arm breech mechanism. The mountings allowed 20° elevation. 14 guns were made for the Navy, the four reserve guns, which were never used, differing in having a sharper taper on the inner 'A' tube. Ten guns were also ordered for the *Almirante Cochrane*, which became the aircraft carrier *Eagle,* and three of these were completed as Mk I for railway mountings, though they were never used in France. The only difference was that the forward slope of the chamber was reduced from 1 in 8 to 1 in 15 to prevent the shell slipping back as the railway mounting allowed 40° elevation.

14in Mk II mounted in the *Abercrombie* class monitors of the First World War, these eight Bethlehem guns were originally intended for the Greek battlecruiser *Salamis.* A further two guns to the same external contours were made by Woolwich and used to regun *Abercrombie.* These latter were of normal wire-wound type, except that the wire only covered the chamber and part of the bore, but the original eight were built up from a thin 'A' tube and three layers, each of three tubes, the first layer reaching the muzzle. The tubes were not efficiently locked together and the guns drooped excessively. The breech bush screwed into the two outer layers and the mechanism, which resembled the Elswick type, was hand-operated. Elevation was 15°.

14in Mk III Two guns built by Elswick for Japan to the Meiji 41st year design and believed to be for the *Yamashiro.* They were altered to give an improved performance identical to that of the 14in Mk I. The main differences from the latter were that they were 1½tons lighter, had Vickers breech mechanisms and an inner 'A' tube with forward shoulders and cannelured rings and were not tapered. They were used in France on railway mountings in 1918.

14in Mk IV Two guns, ex-US Navy, provided as spares for the *Abercrombie* class but never used. Like Mk II but with a very thin inner 'A' tube and with outer tubes properly locked.

	14in Mk I	14in Mk II	14in Mk VI	14in Mk VII
Weight (tons)	84.75	63.1	82	79/79.6
Length oa (in)	648.4	642.45	728	650.85
Length bore (cal)	45	44.5	50.4	45
Chamber (cu in)	23,500	15,115	21,940	22,000
Chamber length (in)	94.165 (I* 93.13)	80.4	110.68	108.54
Projectile (lb)	1586	1400	1586	1590
Charge (lb) – type	344-MD45	355-NCT69 233-MD45 (later)	313-MD45	338.25-SC300 486-SC500 (supercharge)
Muzzle velocity (fs)	2507	2570 2400 (later)	2470	2483 2850(supercharge)
Range (yds)	24,400/20°	19,540/15°, 2500fs	–	38,560/40° 51,200/45° (supercharge)

	15in Mk I	15in Mk II
Weight (tons)	100	97
Length oa (in)	650.4	697
Length bore (cal)	42	45
Chamber (cu in)	30,650	28,000
Chamber length (in)	107.68	–
Projectile (lb)	1920 1938 (later)	– 1938
Charge (lb) – type	428-MD45 432-SC280 (later) 486-SC300 (supercharge)	– 430-SC326
Muzzle velocity (fs)	2467 (1920lb) 2458 (1938lb) 2638 (1938lb, supercharge)	– 2510
Range (yds)	24,350/20°, 30,180/30° (1920lb) 26,650/20°, 33,550/30° (1938lb) 29,930/20°, 37,870/30°, 44,200 max (1938lb supercharge)	– 39,150/40° –

The 14in MkVII guns of the after turret of the battleship *King George V* in 1940.
IWM

14in Mk V Two guns, ex-US Navy, provided as spares for the *Abercrombie* class but never used. Like Mk II but had Asbury roller-cam breech mechanism.

14in Mk VI 24 guns ordered from Vickers by Russia for the *Borodino* class. About 16 guns were completed of which 3, delivered in 1918, were taken over for railway mountings. They were never used in France. Designed for a large-grain nitrocellulose tubular charge, their performance was much degraded with MD cordite. They were of built-up construction – 'A' tube/4 tubes to muzzle/3 tubes/2 tubes/jacket; there was also a short breech ring and the breech bush, which had a small shrunk collar, screwed into the jacket. Vickers-type mechanism was used.

14in Mk VII Mounted in 2 and 4 gun turrets, allowing 40° elevation, in the *King George V* class; also 2 guns on adapted proof mountings for cross-channel firing at Dover. 78 guns were made, including two trial guns. They were of standard built-up construcion, as introduced in the experimental 12in Mk XIV, with tapered inner 'A' tube, 'A' tube, jacket and breech ring, with a shrunk collar on the 'A' tube, the breech bush screwing into the latter. Asbury type mechanism was used. A loose barrel version, Mk VII*, was designed but never made. Supercharges for the 14in Mk VII were only fired by the two Dover guns. The last 46 guns had a different shape of breech ring and weighed 79 tons. A 12.5-ton counterweight was fixed to these and one of 11 tons to the earlier guns so that the centre of gravity was the same. Shells for Mk VII guns had 6/12crh and others nominally 4crh.

Warship pictorial
Breaking-Up HM Ships

by I L Buxton

When ships are being broken up, there is opportunity to take photographs which are impossible to obtain while the ships are in service. Unusual angles from masts and cranes can be obtained while, as demolition proceeds, the arrangement of lower decks, machinery spaces and armament layout is revealed. As a young naval architect, I was particularly interested in the tech nical aspects of warships, so made a number of

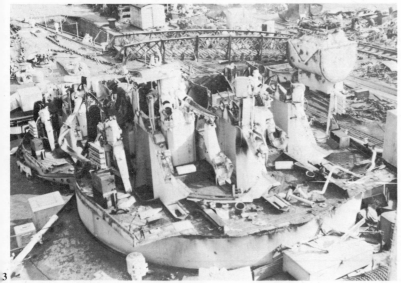

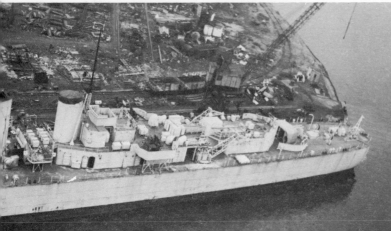

1 A close-up of *King George V*'s bridge, as she is manoeuvred alongside at Dalmuir. All her close-range armament had been removed whilst in reserve. The Mk IV HA directors (the other three survivors had Mk V) are still in their protective 'kooncoting', as is the Type 277 radar aerial on the foremast. The thawing snow has revealed the pattern of some of the structure.

2 A view from *Duke of York*'s foremast head, showing her forward turrets, with their 6in thick roof plates, and the main director with the Type 274 radar aerials above its roof.

3 *Jamaica*'s forward triple 6in turrets, with shields removed, at Dalmuir in August 1961. The round chutes in the floor of the turret are cordite hoists. The shell hoists for the two left guns are in the vertical square structure with loading trays extending aft. One of *Superb*'s condensers lies on the quay.

4 *Gambia*'s after engine room had been opened up by June 1969. The starboard inner steam turbine set is being dismantled. In the foreground is the low-pressure turbine, whose casing incorporated the astern turbine, while in the background is the high-pressure turbine and main gear wheel. The pinion is being lifted past the 2in thick main deck.

5 This jointed view of the fast minelayer *Ariadne* shows her at Dalmuir in February 1965. The embarking hatches for her 156 mines can be seen abreast the fore funnel and abaft the cranes. As with most vessels laid up after the Second World War, the close-range gun barrels have been removed but the actual mountings remain – US twin 40mm and Mk V twin 20mm.

visits to shipbreaking yards from 1956 onwards. At that time, most yards worked on Saturday mornings which, with the co-operation of understanding managements, enabled a wide variety of photographs to be obtained.

This series of photographs includes only those classes which served during the Second World War. Nearly all were taken in Scotland, partly because I was living on the Clyde at the time, but also because Scottish yards broke up the majority of the Royal Navy's larger ships – indeed all its battleships and aircraft carriers. The photographs were all taken with a secondhand 120 camera, mostly without the aid of an exposure meter, and originally processed by myself, but the negatives are still able to produce reasonable prints.

A future pictorial will feature smaller warships.

1 Cut-down amidships to middle deck level (one below the main, armoured, deck level) in November 1959, *Duke of York* reveals the layout of her machinery spaces. The three compartments abreast amidships are: port forward engine room, auxiliary machine room and starboard forward engine room (outer shaft). Forward are the two corresponding boiler rooms; aft the two boiler rooms for the after (inner) shafts and then the two engine rooms, with manoeuvring platform gauges just visible. The large square hole aft is 'Y' turret. magazine space. The bows belong to *Newcastle*, revealing the hoists of 'A' 6in triple turret and the roller path of 'B' turret.

2 The cruiser *Newcastle* at Faslane in August 1959. Although apparently complete, her mainmast and after funnel have already been demolished. The extensive railway tracks at Faslane are a legacy of its original role as wartime Military Port No 1, completed in 1942.

3 The cruiser *Liverpool* was the largest warship broken-up by P & W Maclellan at Bo'ness on the Forth. Seen here in September 1958, she had been in hand for two months. As there was no proper jetty, *Liverpool* was positioned at right angles to the shoreline and demolished from forward by a steam derrick crane erected on her upper deck. As the hulk lightened she was winched up the beach.

4 *Duke of York* reveals her fine lines at Shipbreaking Industries' jetty at Faslane in March 1958. Her final voyage, from her moorings in the Gareloch, was only a mile. Unusually, *Duke of York*'s lighting system was energised below decks for several weeks, making access easier to allow de-equipping of Admiralty stores. Alongside *Duke of York* are the oiler *Rowanol* and the salvage vessel *Salveda*, chartered from the Admiralty by SI's parent company Metal Industries.

5 The reconstructed carrier *Victorious* at Faslane in November 1969. An accidental fire is burning above the hangar deck amidships – a frequent occurrence when using oxy-propane torches which can ignite inflammable material on the opposite side to the cut, or the remnants of any unpumpable fuel still on board. Shipbreaking Industries' 60-ton floating crane was used to remove sections out of reach of the shore cranes.

66

1

2

3

4

5

6

1 *Duke of York* well cut-down in May 1959. The lower section of 'B' turret's ring bulkhead is visible, while the thickness of the 14in to 15in side armour, with its tongued and grooved upper edge, can just be made out. The submarine tucked inside her bows is the Danish *Støren* (ex HMS *Vulpine*) while astern are *Whaddon, Wigtown Bay* and *Ennerdale.* The far jetty and the adjoining land are now incorporated in the submarine base HMS *Neptune.*

2 *Newcastle* well cut-down by January 1960. Forward boiler room uptakes are visible; astern is LST *Vaagso.* In this lightened condition, she is nearly ready to be towed to the nearby beaching ground which dries out at low tide.

3 The name ship of the *King George V* class was the second of the class to go to the shipbreakers. Here, she is arriving at Arnott Young's Dalmuir yard, previously Beardmore's fitting-out basin, one mile downstream from John Brown's Clydebank yard. She had left the Gareloch on 8 January 1958 but lay at Tail of the Bank until 20 January when she was towed by five tugs the last 12 miles.

4 The sterns of the cruiser *Cleopatra* and destroyer *Zebra* at Cashmore's yard, Newport in May 1959. The large tidal range in the River Usk enabled ships to be demolished completely at the one berth without shifting to a finishing berth. *Zebra* had been completely disarmed while in reserve at Devonport.

5 A general view of ships at T W Ward's main yard at Inverkeithing on the Forth in December 1968. From left to right are the cruiser *Gambia,* ferry *Arnhem,* boom defence vessel *Barbican* and destroyer *Broadsword.*

6 The maintenance carrier *Unicorn* at Dalmuir in June 1959. Her high freeboard permitted two 16½ft high hangar decks to be fitted. The stern opening and overhang allowed repaired aircraft to be lowered by overhead crane onto a lighter. The 150 ton hammerhead crane in the background was erected for Beardmore's in 1903 and was of great value in later years as a vantage point from which several of this series of photographs were taken. It has since been demolished.

NEW BOOKS SPRING '81

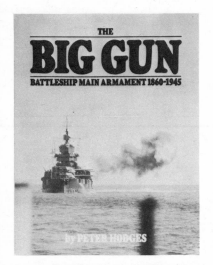

THE BIG GUN
Battleship Main Armament 1860-1945
by Peter Hodges

A history of capital ship main armament from the introduction of the ironclad to the end of the battleship era. The book plots all the major developments in gun mountings from muzzle-loading smooth-bores to the highly sophisticated multi-gunned turrets of the Second World War. While involved in naval gun design, the author had access to official ordnance records and the British side of this book was based on these. However, to complete the story much use has been made of similar sources from other navies, particularly those of Germany and the United States.

10″ × 8″, 144 pages, 75 photographs, 100 line drawings.
ISBN 0 85177 144 0.
Published February 1981. £9.50
(plus £1.25 for postage and packing, when ordering direct).

THE HIDDEN MENACE
Mine warfare, past, present and future
by Maurice Griffiths

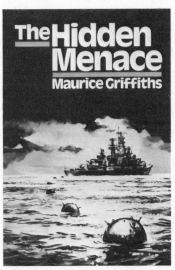

The story of the most sinister of naval weapons, from its primitive beginnings to the current Soviet threat — which includes such science fiction devices as chemical mines to contaminate reservoirs and nuclear mines capable of causing tidal waves.

8½″ × 5½″, 160 pages, 13 line drawings.
ISBN 0 85177 186 6.
Published January 1981. £5.50
(plus £1.00 for postage and packing, when ordering direct).

FROM YOUR LOCAL BOOKSELLER
OR CONWAY MARITIME PRESS LTD, 2 NELSON ROAD, LONDON SE10 9JB

NAVAL BOOKS

Conway Maritime offer an unrivalled range of authoritative and well-illustrated titles on naval subjects. A free catalogue is available, but some of the leading titles are listed below:

Conway's All the World's Fighting Ships 1922-1946

The second in this highly acclaimed series, the 1922-1946 volume covers all significant warships built between the Washington Treaty and the end of the wartime construction programmes. With over 1000 illustrations, it is the ultimate reference book on the navies of World War II.
12¼" × 8½", 464 pages, 506 photos, 530 line drawings. ISBN 0 85177 146 7. £30.00 (plus £2.00 p + p)

The Naval Air War 1939-1945

by Nathan Miller
A highly readable account of naval air forces in action, covering the pilots, their aircraft and carriers, and all the major battles.
9" × 6", 236 pages, 170 photos, 3 maps. ISBN 0 85177 201 3. £8.50 (plus £1.25 p + p)

CONWAY'S ALL THE WORLD'S FIGHTING SHIPS 1860-1905

The first complete listing of all warships between the first ironclad and the *Dreadnought*. "... must rank with the all-time great naval reference works ..." — *The Navy*. "... all the thoroughness and attention to detail we have come to expect from Conway Maritime ... excellent value". — *Ships Monthly*
12¼" × 8½", 448 pages, 471 photos, 506 line drawings. ISBN 0 85177 133 5. £24.00 (plus £2.00 p + p)

BATTLESHIPS OF THE WORLD 1905-1970

by Siegfried Breyer
A spectacular collection of photographs of all capital ships from the *Dreadnought* onwards. "*Battleships of the World* is a lot of book, and it will certainly enthrall all historians, enthusiasts, modellers and general readers alike." — *Airfix Magazine*
11¾" × 8¼", 400 pages, 570 photos, 44 line drawings. ISBN 0 85177 181 5. £25.00 (plus £2.00 p + p)

DESTROYER WEAPONS OF WORLD WAR 2

by Peter Hodges and Norman Friedman
A detailed comparison between British and US destroyer weapons, including mountings, directors and electronics. "... one of the greatest possible additions to the ... range of naval books ..." — *The Navy*
9½" × 7¼", 192 pages, 150 photos, 73 line drawings. ISBN 0 85177 137 8. £7.50 (plus £1.25 p + p)

BATTLESHIP DESIGN AND DEVELOPMENT 1905-1945

by Norman Friedman
The first layman's guide to the design process and the factors governing the development of capital ships. "... an eye-opening study of an extremely complex business ..." — *Nautical Magazine*
10" × 8", 176 pages, 200 photos, plans and line drawings. ISBN 0 85177 135 1. £8.50 (plus £1.25 p + p)

MODERN WARSHIP DESIGN AND DEVELOPMENT

by Norman Friedman
"... never before have the problems and parameters of modern warship design been set out so comprehensively, informatively and clearly ... the book should be read by everyone with a concern for the modern naval scene, professional or amateur, uniformed or civilian." — *Journal of the Royal United Services Institute*
10" × 8", 192 pages, 167 photos, 65 line drawings. ISBN 0 85177 147 5. £9.50 (plus £1.25 p + p)

AIRCRAFT CARRIERS OF THE US NAVY

by Stefan Terzibaschitsch
"... a definitive history of the US carrier fleet from 1920 until the present day ..." — *Journal of the Institute of Marine Engineers*
11¾" × 8¼", 320 pages, 322 photos, 94 plans and line drawings. ISBN 0 85177 159 9. £15.00 (plus £1.50 p + p)

THE AMERICAN FLYING BOAT

by Richard C Knott
A comprehensive history of all such aircraft in the US Navy. "... one of the best aviation books to come from the United States." — *Air Pictorial*
11" × 8½", 262 pages, 123 photos, 5 colour plates, 31 line drawings. ISBN 0 85177 165 3. £15.00 (plus £1.25 p + p)

CAMERA AT SEA 1939-1945

edited by the staff of *Warship*
"A unique collection of some of the best photographs of World War II at sea" — *Sea Power*
12¼" × 8½", 192 pages, 250 photos, 24 colour plates. ISBN 0 85177 124 6. £12.00 (plus £1.50 p + p)

SCALE MODEL WARSHIPS

edited by John Bowen
A complete manual covering every aspect of the hobby. "... a most informative book ..." — *Sea Breezes*
9½" × 7¼", 192 pages, 147 photos, 179 plans and line drawings. ISBN 0 85177 070 X. £7.50 (plus £1.25 p + p)

THE BRITISH SUBMARINE

by Commander F W Lipscomb
A classic history of the British Submarine Service, revised and expanded to include the developments of the nuclear age.
9½" × 7¼", 298 pages, 66 photos, 12 line drawings. ISBN 0 85177 086 X. £6.50 (plus £1.25 p + p)

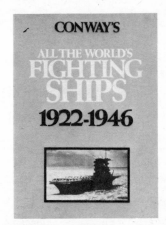